GUATEMALA TRAVEL GUIDE

2024 Edition

Your Ultimate Handbook to Exploring
Hidden Gems, Colors, Flavors, and Wonders
of Guatemala

Jim Baxter

All rights reserved. No part of this book may be reproduced, stored in a retrieval system, or transmitted in any form or by any means, electronic, mechanical, photocopying, recording, or otherwise, without the prior written permission of the copyright owner. The information contained in this book is for general information purposes only. The author and publisher make no representations or warranties of any kind, express or implied, about the completeness, accuracy, reliability, suitability or availability with respect to the book or the information, products, services, or related graphics contained in the book for any purpose. Any reliance you place on such information is therefore strictly at your own risk.

Copyright © 2023 by Jim Baxter.

TABLE OF CONTENT

Introduction

Chapter 1: Guatemala at a Glance

   Geography and Climate

   History and Culture

   People and Language

Chapter 2: Planning Your Trip

   Best Time to Visit

   Entry Requirements and Visa Information

   Transportation and Getting Around

   Accommodation Options

   Safety and Health Tips

Chapter 3: Guatemala City: The Capital's Highlights

   Exploring Historic Zone 1

   Discovering Modern Guatemala City

   Museums and Cultural Centers

   Gastronomy and Nightlife

   La Aurora Zoo: Discovering Wildlife in the Heart of the City

   Plaza Barrios: Immerse in Local Culture and People-Watching

   La Bodeguita del Centro: A Culinary Adventure through Guatemala's Tastes

Chapter 4: Antigua Guatemala: Colonial Charms and Beyond

   The UNESCO World Heritage Site

   Exploring Antigua's Architecture and Churches

   Experiencing Antigua's Markets and Cuisine

   Outdoor Activities and Surrounding Villages

   Antigua's Semana Santa: Witnessing a Spectacular Holy Week Celebration

Museums and Art Galleries: Exploring Antigua's Cultural Heritage

Chapter 5: Lake Atitlán and the Surrounding Villages

　　　Discovering the Enchanting Lake Atitlán

　　　Exploring Indigenous Villages and Traditions

　　　Outdoor Adventures and Water Activities

　　　Spiritual and Wellness Experiences

Chapter 6: Tikal and the Ancient Maya Civilization

　　　Introduction to Tikal National Park

　　　Exploring the Majestic Tikal Ruins

　　　Wildlife and Nature in Tikal

　　　Nearby Archaeological Sites and Natural Parks

Chapter 7: The Pacific Coast and Beach Destinations

　　　Beaches and Surfing Spots

　　　Ecotourism and Wildlife Reserves

　　　Coastal Towns and Fishing Villages

　　　Relaxation and Beachside Activities

Chapter 8: Guatemala's Cultural and Indigenous Heritage

　　　Mayan Traditions and Indigenous Communities

　　　Festivals and Celebrations

　　　Handicrafts and Textiles

　　　Immersion in Local Culture and Traditions

Conclusion

　　　Appendix: Useful Phrases and Vocabulary

Important Notice Before You continue Reading!!!

Step into the pages of this travel guide and prepare for a truly extraordinary experience. Delve into the captivating world of Guatemala, where imagination, creativity, and a thirst for adventure reign supreme. You won't find any images within these pages, as we firmly believe in the power of firsthand exploration, devoid of visual filters or preconceptions. Each monument, every nook and cranny eagerly awaits your arrival, ready to astonish and amaze. Why spoil the thrill of that initial glimpse, that overwhelming sense of wonder? So get ready to embark on an unparalleled journey, where your imagination becomes the sole means of transportation and you, the ultimate guide. Release any preconceived notions and allow yourself to be transported to an authentic Guatemala brimming with hidden treasures. Let the enchantment commence, but remember, the most breathtaking images will be the ones painted by your own eyes.

Unlike many conventional guides, this book needs no detailed maps. Why, you may ask? Because we firmly believe that the truest discoveries happen when you wander, when you surrender to the current of the surroundings and embrace the uncertainty of the path. No rigid itineraries or precise directions are provided here, for we yearn for you to explore Guatemala on your own terms, unbound by limitations or restrictions. Surrender yourself to the currents and unearth hidden gems that no map could reveal. Be audacious, follow your instincts, and brace yourself for serendipitous encounters. The magic of the journey commences now, within a world without maps, where roads materialize with each step and the most extraordinary adventures await in the folds of the unknown.

Introduction

Welcome to Guatemala, the land of eternal spring and a captivating destination nestled in the heart of Central America. This comprehensive travel guide is your key to unlocking the wonders that await you in this culturally rich and visually stunning country. From ancient ruins to volcanic peaks, Guatemala offers a wealth of experiences that will leave you breathless and longing for more.

Guatemala is a country where vibrant colors, fascinating history, and breathtaking landscapes converge to create a tapestry of beauty and intrigue. As you embark on your journey through this enchanting land, you will discover a world of archaeological treasures, colonial architecture, and indigenous traditions that have stood the test of time.

Nature lovers will be enthralled by the diversity of Guatemala's ecosystems, from the lush rainforests teeming with wildlife to the crystal-clear waters of Lake Atitlán and the majestic volcanoes that dot the horizon. Adventure seekers will find their paradise here, with opportunities for hiking, zip-lining, and exploring ancient Mayan ruins hidden deep within the jungles.

But Guatemala is not just about its natural splendor; it is a country that embraces its cultural heritage with pride. You will have the chance to immerse yourself in the traditions and customs of the Mayan people, experience colorful fiestas and religious processions, and admire the intricate handicrafts and textiles created by talented artisans.

In this travel guide, we have curated a wealth of information to help you plan your perfect trip to Guatemala. From practical tips on when to visit and how to navigate the transportation system to recommendations on the best places to stay and dine, we have you covered. Each chapter will take you on a journey through the most iconic and lesser-known destinations, providing you with insider knowledge and local insights to make your experience truly unforgettable.

So, whether you're a history buff, an outdoor enthusiast, a culture seeker, or simply someone in search of a new and exciting adventure, Guatemala has something for everyone. Join us as we delve into the depths of this captivating country, unveiling its hidden gems and immersing ourselves in the magic of Guatemala. Get ready to embark on a journey that will awaken your senses, broaden your horizons, and create memories that will last a lifetime. Let the exploration begin!

Chapter 1: Guatemala at a Glance

Geography and Climate

Guatemala, located in the heart of Central America, is a country blessed with an awe-inspiring and diverse landscape that captures the imagination of travelers from around the world. Surrounded by Mexico to the north and west, Belize to the northeast, Honduras to the east, and El Salvador to the southeast, Guatemala is a captivating land of natural beauty and enchanting destinations.

One of the most remarkable features of Guatemala's geography is its volcanic peaks that adorn the horizon. The country is home to over 30 volcanoes, some of which are still active. These majestic giants shape the topography of Guatemala and contribute to the creation of breathtaking landscapes. From the iconic cone-shaped Volcán de Agua near Antigua to the imposing Acatenango Volcano, which towers over the city of Antigua, these volcanic peaks offer not only stunning views but also opportunities for adventurous hikes and treks.

Beyond the volcanic wonders, Guatemala's landscape is adorned with lush rainforests teeming with diverse flora and fauna. The dense jungles of the Petén region, for instance, are home to the magnificent Maya Biosphere Reserve, a UNESCO World Heritage Site that shelters an incredible array of wildlife and ancient Maya ruins. Exploring the rainforests of Guatemala is an invitation to immerse oneself in nature's embrace, encountering exotic plants, vibrant bird species, and elusive mammals like jaguars and howler monkeys.

The country's geography is also shaped by its expansive lakes, which add a touch of serenity and tranquility to Guatemala's scenery. Lake Atitlán, often referred to as one of the most beautiful lakes in the world, is nestled amidst towering volcanoes and picturesque villages. Its crystal-clear waters reflect the surrounding peaks, creating a magical ambiance that captivates visitors. Lake Petén Itzá, located in the heart of the Maya Biosphere Reserve, offers a unique blend of natural beauty and historical significance, with the archaeological site of Tikal looming nearby.

In addition to its mountain ranges and lakes, Guatemala boasts a stunning coastline along the Pacific Ocean. The country's picturesque beaches and charming coastal towns offer an escape to sun-drenched shores and azure waters. From the black-sand beaches of Monterrico to the palm-fringed shores of Livingston, Guatemala's coastal destinations provide opportunities for relaxation, water sports, and encounters with marine life.

The Sierra Madre mountain range traverses Guatemala from northwest to southeast, defining its topography and contributing to the formation of its diverse landscapes. This mountain range is part of the larger system known as the American Cordillera, which extends along the western side of the Americas. The Sierra Madre creates a dramatic backdrop and serves as a natural boundary between different regions of Guatemala, offering breathtaking vistas and adventurous routes for outdoor enthusiasts.

Standing tall among Guatemala's peaks is Tajumulco, the country's highest volcano and the highest point in Central America, reaching an impressive elevation of 4,220 meters (13,845 feet) above sea level. Climbing Tajumulco is a challenging yet rewarding experience that offers panoramic views of the surrounding landscapes. As the sun rises or sets over the rugged terrain, the beauty of Guatemala unfolds in all its splendor, leaving a lasting impression on those who venture to its summit.

The climate in Guatemala is predominantly tropical, characterized by warm temperatures and high humidity. The country experiences two distinct seasons: the rainy season and the dry season. The rainy season typically spans from May to October, with the heaviest rainfall occurring in June and September. During this time, the landscapes transform into a lush green oasis, with vibrant vegetation and cascading waterfalls. While occasional afternoon showers are common, they often give way to clear skies, allowing travelers to continue their explorations.

The dry season, from November to April, brings drier and milder weather, making it an ideal time for outdoor activities and exploration. During this season, the skies clear up, revealing the stunning landscapes in their full glory. The pleasant temperatures create favorable conditions for hiking, exploring ancient ruins, and indulging in water sports along the coast. Whether you prefer to wander through ancient Maya cities or embark on thrilling adventures, the dry season in Guatemala offers ample opportunities to savor the country's natural beauty.

With its diverse geography and tropical climate, Guatemala beckons travelers to immerse themselves in its captivating landscapes. From the rugged peaks of volcanoes to the verdant rainforests, expansive lakes, and picturesque coastlines, the country offers a myriad of natural wonders waiting to be explored. Guatemala's geography and climate combine to create a paradise for nature enthusiasts, adventure seekers, and cultural enthusiasts alike, making it an unforgettable destination in Central America.

History and Culture

The history of Guatemala is a captivating narrative of ancient civilizations, colonial conquest, and a rich cultural heritage that continues to thrive to this day. One cannot explore Guatemala without encountering the profound influence of the Maya civilization, which flourished in the region for thousands of years.

The Maya civilization, renowned for its advanced architectural and cultural achievements, left behind a legacy of remarkable archaeological sites that serve as windows into the past. Among these sites, Tikal stands as one of the most iconic and awe-inspiring. Located in the dense jungles of northern Guatemala, Tikal was once a thriving city-state and a political, economic, and cultural hub of the Maya world. Its towering pyramids, expansive plazas, and intricately carved stelae offer a glimpse into the grandeur and sophistication of Maya civilization. Visitors to Tikal have the opportunity to wander through the ancient city, surrounded by the sounds of wildlife and the echoes of an ancient civilization.

El Mirador, located in the remote Petén region, is another significant Maya archaeological site. Often referred to as the "Cradle of Maya Civilization," El Mirador boasts monumental structures and the largest pyramid in the Americas, La Danta. Exploring El Mirador requires a sense of adventure as it involves trekking through dense forests and ascending the massive pyramid to witness breathtaking views of the surrounding canopy.

Quiriguá, a UNESCO World Heritage site, showcases intricately carved stelae and monumental sculptures that provide insights into the artistic achievements of the Maya. The stelae depict historical events, royal lineages, and deities, serving as invaluable historical records. Walking among these ancient stone monuments transports visitors to a time long gone, where the Maya thrived and created awe-inspiring works of art.

While the ancient Maya civilization flourished in Guatemala for centuries, the arrival of Spanish conquistadors in the 16th century marked a significant turning point in the country's history. Guatemala, like many other parts of the Americas, became a colony of the Spanish Empire. The impact of Spanish colonization on Guatemala's culture, language, and architecture is still evident today.

Spanish became the dominant language in Guatemala, gradually supplanting the indigenous languages spoken by the Maya. However, the resilience of indigenous cultures is showcased through the preservation of their languages in numerous communities. Today, Guatemala recognizes over 20 indigenous languages, with each language carrying its own unique heritage and contributing to the country's linguistic diversity.

Religion is another aspect deeply influenced by Spanish colonization. Catholicism became the predominant religion, blending with indigenous beliefs and rituals to create a unique syncretic faith. Throughout Guatemala, one can witness the fusion of Catholic traditions with indigenous spirituality in colorful festivals and religious ceremonies. These celebrations, such as the vibrant Semana Santa (Holy Week) processions, showcase the intricate intertwining of indigenous customs and Catholic practices.

Guatemala's cultural heritage is a testament to the blending of its indigenous roots and colonial legacy. The country is renowned for its exquisite craftsmanship, with traditional Mayan textiles, pottery, and woodwork captivating visitors with their intricate designs and vibrant colors. Mayan weavers create intricate textiles using traditional techniques passed down through generations, incorporating symbols and patterns that hold deep cultural significance. Exploring local markets and workshops offers the opportunity to witness these skilled artisans at work and acquire unique, handcrafted pieces that embody Guatemala's cultural richness.

Beyond textiles, Guatemala's artistic heritage extends to ceramics and woodwork. Ceramicists create intricate pottery, often depicting scenes from mythology or everyday life, while woodworkers carve intricate statues, masks, and religious icons. Each piece tells a story and reflects the craftsmanship and creativity of Guatemalan artisans.

Guatemala's cultural tapestry is further enriched by its vibrant festivals and celebrations. From the lively Giant Kite Festival in Sumpango to the sacred rituals of the Day of the Dead in Santiago Sacatepéquez, these events provide a glimpse into the deeply rooted traditions and customs of the Guatemalan people. Participating in these celebrations allows travelers to immerse themselves in the country's cultural fabric, forging connections and gaining a deeper understanding of Guatemala's identity.

People and Language

Guatemala is a nation of rich cultural diversity, with a population that encompasses various ethnic groups. The majority of Guatemalans are of indigenous descent, belonging to different Mayan communities, each with its distinct language, customs, and traditions. This multicultural tapestry contributes to Guatemala's vibrant and unique identity.

Among the most prominent indigenous groups in Guatemala are the K'iche', Kaqchikel, Q'eqchi', Mam, and Xinca, although there are many more throughout the country. These indigenous communities have preserved their ancestral heritage and continue to pass down their traditions from generation to generation. Each group has its own language, which is still actively spoken in their respective regions, allowing for the preservation of linguistic diversity.

The K'iche' people, for example, are one of the largest Mayan groups in Guatemala. They primarily inhabit the highlands of the country and are known for their rich oral tradition, including the Popol Vuh, a sacred Mayan text that recounts the creation of the world. The Kaqchikel people reside in the central highlands and have a distinct language and cultural practices, such as vibrant traditional clothing and ceremonial rituals. The Q'eqchi' people, located in the eastern region, have a strong connection to the land and are known for their agricultural practices and traditional healing methods. The Mam people, concentrated in the western highlands, have a rich artistic heritage, particularly in the field of pottery. The Xinca people, residing in southeastern Guatemala, have a unique cultural identity, distinct from the Mayan groups, and have faced challenges in preserving their traditions due to historical factors.

Despite the diversity among the indigenous groups, they share common threads that weave them together. Respect for nature, a deep spiritual connection, and a strong sense of community are integral aspects of indigenous life in

Guatemala. These values are often reflected in their traditional ceremonies, music, dance, and artwork.

While indigenous communities form a significant portion of Guatemala's population, it's important to note that Spanish is the primary language spoken in the country. Spanish serves as a common means of communication among different ethnic groups and communities, facilitating interactions and fostering unity. It is spoken by the majority of the population, particularly in urban areas and formal settings.

However, the preservation of indigenous languages remains crucial to Guatemala's cultural heritage. Over 20 indigenous languages are still actively spoken in the country, reflecting the linguistic diversity that exists within its borders. These languages act as vessels of cultural identity, allowing indigenous communities to express their unique perspectives, stories, and knowledge systems.

Efforts are being made to promote and revitalize indigenous languages in Guatemala. Bilingual education programs have been implemented in many communities, allowing children to learn their native languages alongside Spanish. Cultural organizations and institutions also play a vital role in preserving and promoting indigenous languages through language documentation, revitalization initiatives, and the production of educational materials.

When visiting Guatemala, one of the most remarkable experiences is the opportunity to interact with the local people. Guatemalans are known for their warmth, hospitality, and strong sense of community. Whether in bustling urban centers or remote rural villages, visitors often encounter the genuine friendliness and welcoming nature of the Guatemalan people.

Interacting with locals provides a unique chance to immerse oneself in Guatemala's rich cultural traditions and gain insights into the way of life in different communities. Engaging in conversations, participating in cultural events, and even staying with indigenous families offer opportunities to forge connections that transcend cultural boundaries. Through these interactions, visitors can learn about traditional practices, such as weaving, pottery making, or traditional medicine, directly from the artisans and practitioners who have inherited these skills from their ancestors.

Furthermore, attending festivals and celebrations allows visitors to witness the vibrancy and diversity of Guatemalan culture firsthand. Festivals are vibrant displays of music, dance, elaborate costumes, and religious rituals, showcasing the fusion of indigenous and Spanish influences. These celebrations often honor patron saints, mark significant agricultural events, or commemorate historical events, providing a glimpse into the cultural tapestry of the nation.

Overall, Guatemala's diverse population, with its indigenous communities and Spanish-speaking majority, offers a captivating blend of cultures, languages, and traditions. Exploring the country's ethnic mosaic provides a deeper understanding of Guatemala's history, heritage, and the rich tapestry of its people. Engaging with the locals offers an opportunity for meaningful cultural exchange, fostering connections that enrich the travel experience and leave lasting memories.

Chapter 2: Planning Your Trip

Best Time to Visit

Guatemala, known as the "Land of Eternal Spring," offers visitors a diverse array of attractions, from ancient ruins and vibrant markets to stunning natural landscapes. To make the most of your trip to Guatemala, it's crucial to consider the timing of your visit. The country experiences a tropical climate with two distinct seasons: the dry season and the rainy season. Understanding the characteristics of each season can help you plan a successful and enjoyable trip.

The dry season in Guatemala typically spans from November to April. This period is widely regarded as the best time to visit the country. During these months, the weather is generally pleasant, with lower chances of rainfall and warmer temperatures. The clear skies and sunny days create an ideal environment for outdoor activities and exploration.

One of the significant advantages of visiting during the dry season is the ease of accessing and exploring archaeological sites. Guatemala is home to several ancient Mayan ruins, such as Tikal, El Mirador, and Yaxhá. These sites are nestled within lush jungles, and visiting them during the dry season means you can navigate the trails and climb the structures with ease. The absence of heavy rainfall ensures that the paths are less muddy and more stable, allowing you to fully immerse yourself in the rich history and architectural marvels of the Mayan civilization.

Furthermore, the dry season presents excellent opportunities for outdoor adventures and nature exploration. Guatemala boasts breathtaking landscapes, including picturesque lakes, towering volcanoes, and dense forests. It's an ideal time for activities like hiking, trekking, and wildlife spotting. The warm temperatures and clear skies create optimal conditions for exploring the scenic beauty of Lake Atitlán, hiking the Pacaya Volcano, or embarking on a jungle tour to spot elusive wildlife species.

Another highlight of the dry season is the vibrant festivals and cultural events that take place throughout Guatemala. From the Semana Santa (Holy Week) celebrations in Antigua to the traditional Mayan ceremonies in indigenous villages, you'll have the chance to witness and participate in the country's rich cultural heritage. The dry season attracts both locals and international visitors, creating a lively atmosphere filled with colorful parades, traditional music, and cultural performances.

While the dry season is undoubtedly the most popular time to visit Guatemala, it's essential to note that the country's diverse geography and microclimates can result in variations in weather conditions. The coastal areas, such as the Pacific and Caribbean coasts, experience a slightly different climate compared to the inland regions. The coastal regions tend to be hotter and more humid year-round, with a higher chance of rainfall. Therefore, it's advisable to pack lightweight and breathable clothing if you plan to explore the coastal areas during the dry season.

On the other hand, the rainy season in Guatemala typically occurs from May to October. This period is characterized by frequent rain showers, particularly in the afternoons and evenings. While the rainy season might deter some travelers, it also has its unique charm and advantages. The landscapes transform into lush greenery, and the rainfall brings life to the flora and fauna. It's a great time for nature enthusiasts and photographers to capture the vibrant colors and dramatic scenery.

During the rainy season, you can expect fewer crowds and lower prices for accommodations and tours. It's an opportunity to explore popular attractions without the bustling crowds and have a more intimate experience with nature. However, it's important to be prepared for the occasional downpours by packing rain gear, waterproof footwear, and protecting electronic devices with waterproof covers.

It's worth noting that the rainy season doesn't necessarily mean continuous rain throughout the day. Mornings often start with clear skies, allowing for outdoor activities and sightseeing. It's advisable to plan your activities accordingly, making the most of the drier mornings and reserving the afternoons for indoor attractions or relaxation.

Entry Requirements and Visa Information

Before embarking on your journey to Guatemala, it's essential to familiarize yourself with the entry requirements and visa information to ensure a smooth and hassle-free travel experience. The entry regulations may vary depending on your nationality and the duration of your stay. Here is a comprehensive guide to help you navigate the entry requirements and visa policies for visiting Guatemala.

Guatemala operates a relatively lenient visa policy, allowing citizens of many countries to enter for tourism purposes without a visa. Travelers from the United States, Canada, the United Kingdom, most European countries, and several other nations are eligible for a visa-free stay of up to 90 days.

This means that you can enter Guatemala as a tourist, stay for up to three months, and explore the country's vibrant culture, natural wonders, and archaeological sites without the need for a visa.

The visa-free entry allows tourists to engage in various activities such as sightseeing, visiting historical sites, experiencing the local cuisine, participating in cultural events, and enjoying outdoor adventures. It's important to note that the visa exemption is specifically for tourism purposes, and any other activities such as business or employment may require a different type of visa or permit.

While citizens of many countries can enjoy visa-free entry, it's always advisable to check the specific visa requirements based on your nationality. Some countries may have bilateral agreements or specific conditions that affect visa policies. The best way to obtain accurate and up-to-date information is to consult with the nearest Guatemalan embassy or consulate or visit the official website of the Ministry of Foreign Affairs of Guatemala.

In addition to the visa requirements, you should also ensure that your passport is valid for at least six months beyond your intended departure date from Guatemala. This is a common requirement in many countries and ensures that you have a valid travel document throughout your stay.

For travelers who wish to extend their stay beyond the initial 90 days, it's possible to apply for an extension at the immigration office in Guatemala. The extension process typically involves submitting an application form, paying a fee, and providing a valid reason for the extension, such as further exploration of the country, volunteering, or studying. It's important to start the extension process well in advance of your initial 90-day period to allow for processing time.

If you plan to engage in activities other than tourism, such as business meetings, attending conferences, or volunteering, it's crucial to check whether you require a different type of visa. Guatemala offers various types of visas, including business visas, work visas, student visas, and others, each with specific requirements and application procedures. It's recommended to consult with the relevant Guatemalan embassy or consulate or seek professional legal advice to determine the appropriate visa category for your specific purpose of travel.

When applying for a visa, it's important to provide all the necessary documentation and meet the specific requirements outlined by the Guatemalan authorities. This may include a completed visa application form, a valid passport, proof of travel insurance, proof of accommodation or hotel reservations, proof of sufficient funds to cover your stay, and a return or onward ticket. It's advisable to check the embassy or consulate website for the most accurate and updated list of requirements to avoid any delays or complications in the visa application process.

It's worth noting that immigration policies and visa requirements can change over time, so it's crucial to stay informed and updated with the latest information before your trip. The Guatemalan embassy or consulate in your country or the official website of the Ministry of Foreign Affairs of Guatemala are reliable sources of information for visa-related queries.

Transportation and Getting Around

Getting around Guatemala requires some planning and understanding of the available transportation options. The country's diverse landscapes, from volcanic peaks to lush rainforests, are best explored by taking advantage of the well-connected network of transportation services. Whether you're traveling between major cities or venturing off the beaten path to remote destinations, Guatemala offers several convenient and reliable modes of transportation.

Domestic Flights:
For travelers looking to cover long distances quickly and efficiently, domestic flights are an excellent option in Guatemala. With several airports scattered across the country, including the main hub at La Aurora International Airport in Guatemala City, domestic air travel provides a convenient and time-saving alternative for those seeking to maximize their exploration of the country.

The availability of domestic flights in Guatemala makes it easy to reach major cities and popular tourist destinations. Domestic airlines such as Avianca, TAG Airlines, and Maya Island Air offer regular flights connecting key locations, including Guatemala City, Flores (the gateway to Tikal), Puerto Barrios, and Quetzaltenango.

Guatemala City, being the capital and largest city, serves as the primary entry point for international travelers. La Aurora International Airport offers numerous domestic flights that connect to various destinations within the country. From here, travelers can quickly and comfortably fly to other major cities or regions without the need for extensive road travel.

One of the popular domestic flight routes in Guatemala is between Guatemala City and Flores. Flores is a small town located near the ancient Maya ruins of Tikal, a UNESCO World Heritage site and one of the country's most iconic attractions. Flying to Flores saves travelers several hours of travel time compared to road transportation, allowing them to optimize their visit to the ancient ruins and explore the surrounding jungle.

In addition to Tikal, domestic flights provide convenient access to other notable destinations. Puerto Barrios, a port city on Guatemala's Caribbean coast, is a gateway to the beautiful beaches and the tropical paradise of Livingston and the Rio Dulce area. Quetzaltenango, often referred to as Xela, is a vibrant city situated in the western highlands of Guatemala and serves as a base for exploring nearby volcanoes, hot springs, and indigenous villages.

Domestic flights are particularly beneficial for travelers with limited time who want to experience the diverse landscapes and cultural treasures of Guatemala efficiently. By taking advantage of air travel, visitors can reduce travel time and maximize their opportunities for exploration and immersion in the country's rich heritage.

When considering domestic flights, it's essential to keep in mind a few practical tips:

- Booking in Advance: To secure the best fares and ensure availability, it is advisable to book domestic flights in advance, especially during peak travel seasons or holidays.

- Luggage Restrictions: Domestic airlines in Guatemala often have specific luggage restrictions, including weight limits and restrictions on the number of bags allowed. It's crucial to check these requirements before your flight to avoid any additional fees or complications.

- Check-In and Security Procedures: Arriving at the airport with sufficient time before your flight is important to complete the check-in and security procedures smoothly. It is recommended to arrive at least one to two hours before your domestic flight departure time.

- Airport Transfers: When traveling to and from airports, it is advisable to arrange transportation in advance to ensure a seamless journey. Many airports offer transportation options such as taxis or private shuttles that can take you to your final destination.

While domestic flights in Guatemala offer speed and convenience, it's important to note that they may not always be the most cost-effective option, particularly for shorter distances or if you have more time to explore. Depending on your travel preferences, budget, and itinerary, it may be worthwhile to consider a combination of domestic flights and other modes of transportation, such as buses or private shuttles, to create a well-rounded travel experience.

Ultimately, domestic flights in Guatemala provide a valuable transportation option for travelers seeking efficiency, convenience, and the opportunity to cover long distances swiftly. By incorporating domestic air travel into your itinerary, you can optimize your time, visit multiple destinations, and make the most of your journey through the captivating landscapes and vibrant culture of Guatemala.

Buses:

Buses are the backbone of Guatemala's transportation system, offering a reliable, extensive, and affordable mode of travel. With a well-established network of routes, buses connect cities, towns, and even remote villages across the country, providing access to both popular tourist destinations and off-the-beaten-path locations.

The bus terminals, known as "puertas" or "central camionera," serve as hubs where buses depart and arrive. Major cities like Guatemala City and Antigua have large bus terminals that act as transportation hubs, connecting various regions of the country. From these terminals, travelers can access buses heading to different destinations throughout Guatemala.

One of the unique aspects of bus travel in Guatemala is the iconic long-distance buses, often referred to as "chicken buses." These buses are vibrant, colorfully decorated vehicles that were once used as school buses in the United States. After being retired from service, they are imported to Guatemala and undergo extensive modifications to accommodate passengers and luggage.

The charm of the chicken buses lies not only in their eye-catching appearance but also in the cultural experience they offer. These buses are a budget-friendly option for traveling between major cities and tourist destinations. They provide an opportunity to immerse yourself in the local atmosphere, as they are often packed with Guatemalan commuters, street vendors, and sometimes even musicians. The lively ambiance and interactions with locals make riding a chicken bus an adventure in itself.

While the chicken buses offer a unique cultural experience, it's important to be aware of a few considerations. These buses can get crowded, especially during peak travel times, and it's not uncommon for passengers to stand in the aisles. As such, it's advisable to secure your belongings and keep an eye on your personal belongings throughout the journey.

Furthermore, the schedules of chicken buses may not always be punctual. Delays can occur due to various factors such as traffic congestion or road conditions. Therefore, it's recommended to plan your travel itinerary with some flexibility and allocate extra time for unforeseen delays.

In addition to long-distance buses, Guatemala also has a network of local buses that cater to shorter distances within cities and towns. These smaller buses are a convenient option for exploring a specific area or reaching nearby attractions. Compared to long-distance buses, local buses are generally less crowded, providing a more comfortable travel experience for shorter journeys.

Local buses are particularly useful for navigating urban areas like Guatemala City or Antigua, allowing you to explore different neighborhoods and visit popular sights. They are also a practical option for reaching nearby markets, archaeological sites, or natural attractions located within a city or town.

When using buses in Guatemala, it's advisable to have small change on hand for purchasing tickets. The fare is typically paid directly to the bus driver or conductor upon boarding the bus. Additionally, it's helpful to have a basic understanding of Spanish, as bus announcements and signage are primarily in the local language.

Private Shuttles:
Private shuttles are a popular choice for travelers seeking more comfort, convenience, and personalized travel experiences. They are particularly common for transportation between popular tourist destinations, such as Antigua, Lake Atitlán, and Tikal. Private shuttles offer door-to-door service and can be arranged through tour operators, hotels, or transportation companies. They provide the flexibility to set your own schedule and make stops along the way for sightseeing or photo opportunities. Private shuttles

are available in various sizes, accommodating different group sizes and luggage requirements.

Taxis:
Taxis are widely available in Guatemala, particularly in urban areas. They are a convenient option for short distances within cities or for transportation to and from airports. In larger cities like Guatemala City, there are traditional taxis that can be hailed on the street or called through taxi services. It's advisable to use licensed taxis or those recommended by your accommodation to ensure safety and fair pricing. In tourist areas, you may also find "remises," which are private taxis that can be hired for longer distances or day trips.

When using taxis, it's important to establish the fare or use a meter if available before starting the journey to avoid any potential misunderstandings. It's also recommended to carry smaller bills as taxi drivers may not always have change for larger denominations.

Rental Cars:
For travelers seeking greater independence and flexibility, renting a car is an option worth considering. Rental car agencies are available in major cities and at airports. However, it's important to note that driving in Guatemala can be challenging, particularly for those unfamiliar with local traffic conditions and road infrastructure. Guatemalan roads can vary in quality, and driving styles may differ from what you're accustomed to. It's essential to exercise caution, follow traffic rules, and be prepared for unexpected situations. Additionally, some rental car agencies may require an international driver's license or a minimum age for renting a car, so it's advisable to check the specific requirements in advance.

When planning your transportation in Guatemala, it's helpful to consider a few additional tips:

1. Research and plan your routes in advance, especially for long-distance journeys or trips to remote areas. Understand the distances, travel times, and any potential road conditions or construction that may affect your journey.
2. Be prepared for occasional delays or schedule changes, particularly when using public transportation. It's advisable to build in some buffer time to account for unforeseen circumstances.
3. If you're not comfortable navigating the local transportation system or prefer the convenience of organized tours, consider booking guided tours or private drivers through reputable tour operators or your accommodation.
4. Always keep your belongings secure and within sight, especially when traveling on buses or in crowded areas. Be vigilant and aware of your surroundings to prevent theft or loss of personal items.
5. If you're traveling to rural or off-the-beaten-path destinations, it's advisable to check the availability of transportation options in advance. Some areas may have limited or irregular transport services, requiring additional planning or arranging private transportation.

When it comes to obtaining information on transportation in Guatemala, several popular apps can be helpful in planning and navigating your journey. Here are some widely used apps that provide transportation information in Guatemala:

- Uber: Uber operates in major cities in Guatemala, including Guatemala City and Antigua. The app allows you to book rides with registered drivers, providing a convenient and reliable transportation option.

- Moovit: Moovit is a comprehensive transit app that covers public transportation systems in many cities worldwide, including Guatemala City. It provides real-time bus schedules, routes, and trip planning features, making it easier to navigate the local bus network.

- Google Maps: Google Maps is a versatile app that offers detailed maps, turn-by-turn directions, and estimated travel times. It also provides public transportation information, including bus routes and schedules in Guatemala City and some other urban areas.

- GuateBus: GuateBus is a dedicated app specifically designed for navigating the bus system in Guatemala City. It provides real-time information on bus routes, schedules, and estimated arrival times.

- Cabify: Similar to Uber, Cabify is another ride-hailing app available in Guatemala. It allows you to request private car services with professional drivers in selected cities, offering an alternative to traditional taxis.

- Waze: Waze is a community-based navigation app that provides real-time traffic updates, road conditions, and the fastest route options. It's particularly useful for driving in Guatemala, helping you navigate through congested areas and find the most efficient routes.

- TransMetro GT: TransMetro GT is an app specifically designed for the Transmetro system in Guatemala

City. It provides real-time information on routes, bus schedules, and station locations, making it easier to utilize this efficient mass transit system.

It's worth noting that while these apps can be valuable resources, connectivity and availability of services may vary in different areas of Guatemala. Additionally, it's advisable to have a backup plan and be prepared with offline maps or physical copies of bus schedules in case of limited internet access or unforeseen circumstances.

Remember to exercise caution and prioritize your safety when using transportation apps. Verify driver details, confirm vehicle information, and always share your trip details with a trusted person for added security.

By utilizing these popular transportation apps, you can enhance your travel experience in Guatemala by efficiently planning your journeys, accessing real-time information, and making informed transportation choices.

By understanding and utilizing the available transportation options in Guatemala, you can navigate the country with ease and make the most of your travel experience. Whether you choose domestic flights, buses, private shuttles, taxis, or rental cars, each mode of transport offers its own advantages and allows you to explore the diverse beauty and rich culture that Guatemala has to offer.

Accommodation Options

Guatemala offers a diverse range of accommodation options that cater to the preferences and budgets of all types of travelers. Whether you're seeking luxury, immersion in local culture, or budget-friendly stays, you'll find suitable choices throughout the country.

In cities like Guatemala City and Antigua, visitors have access to a wide array of accommodation options. Luxury hotels provide a high level of comfort and amenities, ensuring a luxurious and pampering experience for guests. These establishments often boast elegant interiors, spacious rooms, top-notch service, and facilities such as swimming pools, spas, fitness centers, and gourmet restaurants. Many luxury hotels in Guatemala City and Antigua are part of renowned international chains, ensuring a consistent standard of quality and service.

For travelers looking for a more intimate and authentic experience, boutique guesthouses are an excellent choice. These smaller-scale accommodations offer personalized service and unique character. Often located in historic buildings or charming neighborhoods, boutique guesthouses provide a cozy and welcoming atmosphere. Guests can expect stylish rooms, tasteful decor, and a sense of local charm. The hosts of these establishments are often passionate about showcasing the local culture and are eager to share insider tips and recommendations with their guests.

One of the distinctive accommodation options in Guatemala is staying in colonial-style hotels or bed and breakfasts. Antigua, in particular, is renowned for its beautifully restored colonial buildings that have been transformed into boutique hotels and bed and breakfasts. These establishments exude a historic charm, with courtyard gardens, colorful facades, and traditional architecture. Staying in a colonial-style hotel allows guests to immerse themselves in the city's rich history while enjoying modern comforts. Many of these properties feature individually decorated rooms, traditional furnishings, and excellent dining options.

In rural areas and smaller towns across Guatemala, budget-friendly accommodation options are readily available. Hostels are a popular choice for backpackers and budget-conscious travelers. These establishments typically offer dormitory-style rooms with shared facilities, creating a social and communal atmosphere. Hostels are a great way to meet fellow travelers, exchange travel tips, and forge new friendships. Some hostels also provide private rooms for those seeking a bit more privacy.

Guesthouses are another affordable option, particularly in smaller towns and villages. These family-run establishments offer a cozy and welcoming environment, often with simple yet comfortable rooms. Guesthouses provide an opportunity to interact with local hosts, who can offer insights into the local culture, traditions, and attractions.

For nature enthusiasts and eco-conscious travelers, Guatemala offers a range of eco-lodges nestled in pristine natural surroundings. These eco-lodges are designed to minimize their environmental impact while providing guests with a unique and immersive experience. Located in areas of natural beauty, such as national parks, rainforests, or near volcanoes, eco-lodges allow guests to connect with nature. They often offer rustic yet comfortable accommodations, blending seamlessly with the natural environment. Activities such as hiking, birdwatching, wildlife spotting, and sustainability-focused initiatives are typically available.

For those seeking even more unique experiences, camping and homestays with indigenous communities are possible in Guatemala. Camping grounds can be found in various national parks and natural reserves, providing an opportunity to sleep under the stars and be close to nature. Homestays allow visitors to live with local families, experiencing their way of life, traditions, and customs firsthand. This immersive experience enables travelers to forge meaningful connections, gain insights into indigenous cultures, and contribute to the local communities.

Additionally, Guatemala's diverse range of accommodation options allows visitors to tailor their stay to specific interests and activities. For example, if you're a history enthusiast exploring the ancient Mayan ruins scattered throughout the country, staying in a colonial-style hotel in Antigua or near archaeological sites such as Tikal can transport you back in time. These accommodations often showcase elements of the region's rich cultural heritage, allowing you to immerse yourself in the historical ambiance.

On the other hand, if you're an adventure seeker looking to conquer the country's volcanic peaks or embark on thrilling outdoor activities, eco-lodges and camping grounds provide convenient access to these natural wonders. Imagine waking up to the sounds of the rainforest, surrounded by lush greenery, as you prepare for a day of hiking, zip-lining, or exploring hidden waterfalls. The eco-lodges in Guatemala are designed to harmonize with the environment, offering a sustainable and eco-friendly way to experience the country's remarkable biodiversity.

For those seeking cultural exchange and a deeper understanding of local traditions, homestays with indigenous communities are an extraordinary opportunity. Guatemala is home to numerous indigenous groups, each with its distinct customs, language, and way of life. By staying with a host family, you'll gain firsthand knowledge of their traditions, partake in traditional activities, and savor authentic homemade meals. The warmth and hospitality of the Guatemalan people will undoubtedly leave a lasting impression on your journey.

It's worth noting that regardless of the type of accommodation you choose, Guatemala's hospitality industry prioritizes responsible and sustainable practices. Many hotels and lodges implement eco-friendly initiatives such as recycling programs, energy-saving measures, and support for local communities. By selecting accommodation that aligns with your values, you can contribute to the preservation of Guatemala's natural and cultural heritage.

When planning your trip, it's advisable to book your accommodations in advance, especially during peak travel seasons or popular festivals. This ensures you secure your preferred choice and allows for better planning of your itinerary. Online travel platforms, hotel booking websites, and local travel agencies are valuable resources for finding and comparing accommodation options in different regions of Guatemala.

Before making your final decision, consider factors such as location, accessibility to attractions and transportation hubs, amenities and services provided, and reviews from previous guests. By doing your research and understanding your own travel preferences and budget, you can find the perfect accommodation that enhances your experience and makes your stay in Guatemala truly unforgettable.

When it comes to finding and booking accommodation in Guatemala, there are several popular apps and websites that travelers commonly use. These platforms provide a convenient way to explore various options, compare prices, read reviews, and make reservations. Here are some of the popular apps and websites for finding and booking accommodation in Guatemala:

- Airbnb: Airbnb is a widely used platform that allows individuals to rent out their homes, apartments, or rooms to travelers. It offers a range of accommodation options, including entire homes, private rooms, and shared spaces. Airbnb provides filters to narrow down your search based on location, price range, amenities, and property type.

- Booking.com: Booking.com is a popular online travel agency that offers a wide selection of hotels, resorts, guesthouses, and other types of accommodations in Guatemala. The platform allows you to search by location, dates, and specific preferences. It provides detailed information about each property, including photos, reviews, and amenities, making it easier to compare options and make reservations.

- Expedia: Expedia is another well-known online travel agency that offers a variety of accommodation options in Guatemala. It provides a user-friendly interface to search and book hotels, resorts, and other types of lodging. Expedia often offers package deals that include both flights and accommodations, allowing travelers to save money by bundling their bookings.

- Hotels.com: Hotels.com is a popular hotel booking website that features a wide range of hotels and resorts in Guatemala. The platform offers filters to refine your search based on location, price, star rating, and amenities. Hotels.com also has a loyalty program that rewards frequent travelers with free nights and exclusive discounts.

- TripAdvisor: TripAdvisor is a well-established travel platform that provides comprehensive information and user-generated reviews of accommodations in Guatemala. It allows you to search for hotels, bed and breakfasts, and vacation rentals, while also providing insights into nearby attractions, restaurants, and activities. TripAdvisor's user reviews can be helpful in assessing the quality and suitability of different accommodations.

- Hostelworld: For budget travelers or those seeking a social atmosphere, Hostelworld is a popular platform for finding and booking hostels in Guatemala. It offers a wide selection of budget-friendly accommodations with dormitory-style rooms and communal facilities. Hostelworld provides detailed information about each property, including reviews, ratings, and availability.

- Agoda: Agoda is an online travel agency that specializes in offering accommodation options in Asia, but it also includes properties in other parts of the world, including Guatemala. The platform provides a variety of lodging choices, including hotels, resorts, and guesthouses. Agoda often features special deals and discounts for travelers.

These apps and websites offer convenience and flexibility in finding and booking accommodation in Guatemala. It's recommended to compare prices, read reviews, and consider the location and amenities that best suit your needs before making a reservation. Additionally, it's always a good idea to contact the accommodation directly if you have any specific questions or special requests.

In summary, Guatemala offers a wide range of accommodation options that cater to every traveler's preferences and budget. From luxury hotels and boutique guesthouses to colonial-style hotels and bed and breakfasts, budget-friendly hostels and guesthouses, eco-lodges in natural settings, camping grounds, and immersive homestays with indigenous communities, the country ensures that there is something for everyone. By selecting the right accommodation, you can enhance your journey, whether it's through luxury and comfort, cultural immersion, eco-consciousness, or unique experiences that connect you with the country's rich history, natural beauty, and vibrant traditions.

Safety and Health Tips

When traveling to any destination, prioritizing safety and health should always be a top concern. Guatemala, like many countries, offers a wonderful and enriching travel experience, but it's important to take certain precautions to ensure a safe and enjoyable trip. While Guatemala is generally a safe country to visit, it's always advisable to be prepared and proactive in safeguarding your well-being. Here are some essential tips to consider for a safe and healthy journey:

Obtain Travel Insurance:
One of the most important steps in trip planning is to secure comprehensive travel insurance that covers medical emergencies and evacuation if necessary. In the event of an unexpected illness, injury, or any other medical emergency, having travel insurance can provide peace of mind and financial protection.

Stay Informed about Safety Situation:
Before traveling to Guatemala, it's essential to stay informed about the current safety situation in the country. While most popular tourist areas are generally safe, it's advisable to keep track of any potential risks or safety advisories, particularly in more remote or rural areas. Checking travel advisories issued by your home country's government and consulting reliable travel resources can help you make informed decisions about your itinerary.

Follow Local Advice:
When in Guatemala, it's crucial to follow the advice and recommendations of local authorities and trusted sources. Keep yourself updated on any security alerts or changes in the local situation. Local authorities are usually the best source of information regarding safety, particularly in areas where political or social unrest may occur.

Be Cautious of Your Surroundings:
Maintaining awareness of your surroundings is important in any destination. Avoid displaying valuable items such as expensive jewelry, cameras, or smartphones in crowded or public areas. Pickpocketing can occur in busy tourist areas, so it's recommended to keep your belongings secure and be vigilant of your personal belongings at all times. Using a discreet and secure money belt or bag can be helpful in keeping your valuables safe.

Use Reliable Transportation Services:
When getting around in Guatemala, it's advisable to use reliable transportation services. Opt for licensed taxis or reputable transportation companies, particularly when traveling late at night or in unfamiliar areas. If possible, book transportation in advance or seek recommendations from trusted sources to ensure a safe and reliable journey.

Consult with a Healthcare Professional:
Prior to your trip, it's recommended to consult with a healthcare professional or travel medicine specialist to receive any necessary vaccinations or medications. Discuss your travel plans, including the specific regions you intend to visit, and inquire about any recommended vaccinations or preventive measures to protect against diseases such as malaria, dengue fever, or typhoid. It's also a good

opportunity to ensure that you are up to date on routine vaccinations.

Carry a First Aid Kit:
Pack a basic first aid kit containing essential medical supplies, such as bandages, antiseptic cream, pain relievers, and any prescribed medications you regularly take. It's always better to be prepared for minor injuries or illnesses, especially if you plan on engaging in outdoor activities or exploring remote areas where medical facilities may be limited.

Practice Hygiene and Food Safety:
Maintaining good hygiene and food safety practices is crucial for staying healthy during your trip to Guatemala. Wash your hands frequently, especially before meals and after using public facilities. Drink only bottled or purified water, and avoid consuming raw or undercooked food, as well as street food from unhygienic stalls. It's also advisable to peel fruits and vegetables or wash them thoroughly with safe water before eating.

Respect Local Customs and Traditions:
Respecting local customs and traditions is not only important for cultural sensitivity but also for your own safety. Familiarize yourself with the local customs, dress modestly when visiting religious sites, and follow any specific guidelines or instructions provided by local communities or authorities.

By following these safety and health tips, you can minimize risks and ensure a smooth and enjoyable journey in Guatemala. Remember, being well-prepared and informed allows you to fully immerse yourself in the country's rich culture, breathtaking landscapes, and unforgettable experiences while prioritizing your well-being.

Chapter 3: Guatemala City: The Capital's Highlights

Exploring Historic Zone 1

Overview of Zone 1: The Historical Heart of Guatemala City

As you step into Historic Zone 1 of Guatemala City, you are transported back in time to the origins of the capital. This area, also known as "Centro Histórico" or "Casco Viejo," is the historical heart of the city and showcases the rich architectural and cultural heritage of Guatemala. With its narrow cobblestone streets and well-preserved colonial buildings, Zone 1 offers a captivating glimpse into the city's past.

Architectural Gems: Discovering Colonial Buildings and Landmarks

Zone 1 is a treasure trove of colonial-era architecture, offering a captivating glimpse into Guatemala's history. As you wander through its streets, you'll encounter numerous architectural gems that have stood the test of time.

One notable example is the Palacio del Ayuntamiento (City Hall), an exquisite colonial-style building that showcases intricate detailing and a majestic facade. Its grand presence is a testament to the city's governance and administration.

Another iconic landmark is the Edificio de Correos (Post Office Building), a striking neoclassical structure adorned with elaborate sculptures and elegant columns. The building's historical significance and architectural beauty make it a must-see for architecture enthusiasts.

Other notable colonial buildings in Zone 1 include the Iglesia Yurrita, a beautiful church known for its stunning bell tower, and the Palacio del Capitán General, an imposing structure that once served as the residence of the Spanish governors.

Plaza Mayor: Exploring the Main Square and its Surroundings

The Plaza Mayor, the main square of Guatemala City, serves as the beating heart of Zone 1. It's a gathering place for locals and visitors, where you can soak up the lively atmosphere and witness the pulse of the city.

Surrounding the plaza, you'll find a variety of shops, cafes, and restaurants. Take a leisurely stroll and explore the charming alleys that branch off from the square, revealing hidden gems and inviting storefronts.

At the center of the Plaza Mayor stands a monument dedicated to the country's national hero, Miguel Hidalgo. This iconic statue serves as a reminder of Guatemala's struggle for independence and symbolizes the indomitable spirit of its people.

The Plaza Mayor is also a venue for cultural events and celebrations throughout the year. From live music performances to traditional dance exhibitions, there's always something happening in this vibrant square.

National Palace: Unveiling Guatemala's Political Center

The National Palace (Palacio Nacional) is an architectural masterpiece that commands attention with its grandeur and historical significance. This iconic building serves as the seat of the Guatemalan government and is a symbol of the country's political power and heritage.

As you approach the National Palace, you'll be captivated by its neoclassical design and the intricately carved stone facade. The entrance is guarded by the Presidential Honor Guard, adding to the sense of grandeur and importance.

While access to the interior is restricted, visitors can admire the exterior and take in the symbolic elements that adorn the building. El Torre del Reloj (The Clock Tower) is a notable feature, and its bells chime to mark the passing of time.

The National Palace is not only a symbol of political authority but also a testament to Guatemala's historical journey. It stands as a reminder of the country's struggles and triumphs, making it a significant landmark in Zone 1.

Metropolitan Cathedral: A Symbol of Faith and Heritage

The Metropolitan Cathedral (Catedral Metropolitana) is a majestic structure that dominates the skyline of Zone 1. With its imposing twin towers and intricate architectural details, it stands as a symbol of faith and cultural heritage.

The construction of the cathedral began in the late 18th century and took several decades to complete. It reflects a blend of architectural styles, including Spanish Baroque and Mudejar influences.

Step inside the Metropolitan Cathedral, and you'll be greeted by a tranquil ambiance and a sense of reverence. The interior boasts stunning altars, religious paintings, and intricately carved wooden details. The spiritual significance and artistic beauty of the cathedral create an atmosphere of contemplation and awe.

The cathedral's central nave leads to the Capilla del Santo Hermano Pedro, a chapel dedicated to Guatemala's first saint. This sacred space attracts pilgrims and devotees who come to pay their respects and seek solace.

Mercado Central: Immersing in the Vibrant Market Culture

Mercado Central is a bustling market that encapsulates the vibrant spirit of Guatemala City. It's a sensory experience like no other, where the sights, sounds, and scents merge to create a vibrant tapestry of local culture.

As you enter Mercado Central, you'll find yourself surrounded by a kaleidoscope of colors from the vibrant displays of fresh fruits, vegetables, and flowers. The market is a hub for local vendors, artisans, and craftsmen, showcasing their wares and creating a lively atmosphere.

Stroll through the narrow aisles, and you'll discover a multitude of stalls offering a wide array of products, from traditional textiles and handicrafts to spices, herbs, and medicinal plants. It's the perfect place to find unique souvenirs and immerse yourself in the local shopping scene.

The market is also a culinary haven, with numerous food stalls and small eateries serving up mouthwatering Guatemalan dishes. Don't miss the opportunity to savor traditional favorites such as tamales, chuchitos, and atol, and wash it down with a cup of freshly brewed Guatemalan coffee.

Mercado Central is not just a place to shop and eat—it's a cultural experience that allows you to connect with the local community and witness the daily rhythm of Guatemalan life. Engage in friendly conversations with vendors, learn about their products and traditions, and embrace the lively energy that permeates the market.

Exploring Historic Zone 1 in Guatemala City is a captivating journey through Guatemala's history, architecture, and vibrant culture. From the colonial buildings and landmarks that stand as testament to the city's heritage to the bustling Plaza Mayor and the vibrant Mercado Central, each corner of Zone 1 offers unique experiences and insights.

As you wander through the streets, take the time to appreciate the architectural marvels and the stories they tell. Explore the main square and its surroundings, immersing yourself in the bustling atmosphere and witnessing the pulse of the city. Unveil the grandeur of the National Palace and its political significance, and soak in the spiritual ambiance of the Metropolitan Cathedral.

Finally, lose yourself in the vibrant market culture of Mercado Central, where you can engage with local vendors, sample traditional flavors, and bring home a piece of Guatemalan craftsmanship.

Zone 1 is a living testament to Guatemala's past and present, a place where history, culture, and tradition converge. So, set out on your journey of exploration, and let the captivating charm of Historic Zone 1 unfold before your eyes, leaving you with cherished memories and a deeper appreciation for Guatemala's capital city.

Discovering Modern Guatemala City

Modern Guatemala City, also known as Guatemala City (or "Guate" as locals affectionately call it), is a bustling metropolis that perfectly blends urban development, cultural richness, and natural beauty. While it may not have the same colonial charm as its neighboring city, Antigua Guatemala, it has its own unique appeal and a vibrant energy that captivates visitors.

With a history dating back to its founding in 1776, modern Guatemala City has evolved into a dynamic center for commerce, arts, and entertainment. Once a city known for its concrete jungle, it has undergone significant transformations in recent years, embracing contemporary architectural designs, green initiatives, and a focus on cultural development.

Paseo de la Reforma: Strolling through the Urban Boulevard

One of the iconic landmarks of modern Guatemala City is Paseo de la Reforma. This urban boulevard stretches for several kilometers and is lined with towering buildings, parks, and sculptures. Walking along Paseo de la Reforma allows you to experience the city's vibrant atmosphere, witness its architectural diversity, and take in the sights and sounds of daily life.

As you stroll down Paseo de la Reforma, you'll encounter modern office complexes, luxurious hotels, trendy cafes, and bustling street vendors. The boulevard is also home to several important government buildings, including the National Palace and the Supreme Court of Justice. Admire the blend of contemporary and classical architectural styles, showcasing the city's ongoing development and preservation of its historical roots.

Zona Viva: The Entertainment and Commercial District

Located in the heart of modern Guatemala City, Zona Viva is the city's premier entertainment and commercial district. It's a lively hub that comes alive day and night, offering an array of dining options, nightclubs, bars, theaters, and shopping opportunities.

Zona Viva is a popular gathering place for locals and tourists alike, known for its vibrant nightlife scene. Whether you're seeking a lively nightclub to dance the night away, a cozy bar to enjoy a cocktail, or a theater to catch a live performance, Zona Viva has it all. The district hosts cultural events, concerts, and festivals throughout the year, showcasing the city's artistic and musical talents.

During the day, Zona Viva transforms into a bustling commercial center, with upscale boutiques, international brand stores, and shopping malls. From fashion and accessories to home decor and souvenirs, you'll find a diverse range of shops catering to different tastes and budgets. Indulge in a session of retail therapy, exploring the latest fashion trends or discovering unique Guatemalan handicrafts to take home as mementos.

Shopping Centers and Boutiques: Retail Therapy in Guatemala City

Beyond Zona Viva, modern Guatemala City is dotted with shopping centers and boutiques that cater to various preferences and budgets. Whether you're looking for international brands or locally crafted products, the city offers a plethora of options.

Oakland Mall, located in Zone 10, is one of the most popular shopping centers in the city. This modern complex features a wide range of stores, including high-end fashion brands, electronics, home goods, and a diverse selection of restaurants and cafes. It also offers entertainment options such as movie theaters and children's play areas, making it a one-stop destination for leisure and shopping.

For those seeking a more local experience, Mercado de Artesanías located in Zone 13 is a must-visit. This vibrant market is a treasure trove of traditional handicrafts, textiles, pottery, and other artisanal products. Here, you can immerse yourself in Guatemala's rich cultural heritage, interacting with local artisans, and finding unique pieces that reflect the country's artistic traditions.

Parks and Green Spaces: Finding Serenity Amidst the Bustle

While modern Guatemala City is known for its urban development, it also offers several parks and green spaces where visitors can find respite from the hustle and bustle of city life. These oases of tranquility provide opportunities to relax, enjoy nature, and engage in recreational activities.

One such park is the Metropolitan Park, located in Zone 13. Spanning over 7,200 acres, it is the largest urban park in

Central America. The park features hiking and biking trails, picnic areas, and breathtaking viewpoints that offer panoramic views of the city and surrounding mountains. It's a perfect spot for outdoor enthusiasts, families, and nature lovers.

La Aurora Zoo, situated within the boundaries of the Metropolitan Park, combines the beauty of wildlife with the convenience of an urban setting. The zoo is home to a diverse range of animals, including exotic species from around the world. Visitors can observe and learn about these creatures while strolling through well-designed enclosures. The zoo also focuses on education and conservation, with interactive exhibits and programs that raise awareness about biodiversity and wildlife preservation.

Residential Neighborhoods: Exploring Local Life and Architecture

To truly experience the essence of modern Guatemala City, it's worth venturing beyond the tourist hotspots and exploring its diverse residential neighborhoods. Each neighborhood has its own unique charm, architectural styles, and local character.

Zone 4, also known as "Zona 4," is an up-and-coming neighborhood that has undergone a revitalization in recent years. It is known for its colorful street art, trendy cafes, and bohemian atmosphere. Take a leisurely walk along its streets, stopping by local galleries, independent shops, and hidden gems that showcase the city's vibrant art scene.

Zone 15, on the other hand, offers a glimpse into the city's contemporary architectural designs and upscale residential areas. Here, you'll find modern apartment complexes, gated communities, and spacious parks. It's a neighborhood that exudes a sense of exclusivity and tranquility, providing a contrast to the bustling city center.

As you explore these residential neighborhoods, take the opportunity to interact with locals, visit local markets, and try authentic cuisine at neighborhood eateries. This will give you a deeper understanding of the city's culture, traditions, and the everyday lives of its residents.

Modern Guatemala City is a vibrant and evolving metropolis that offers a wide range of experiences for visitors. From strolling along the urban boulevard of Paseo de la Reforma to immersing yourself in the entertainment and commercial district of Zona Viva, there is always something to discover. Whether you're indulging in retail therapy at shopping centers and boutiques, finding serenity in parks and green spaces, or exploring the diverse residential neighborhoods, modern Guatemala City is a destination that combines the conveniences of urban life with a rich cultural tapestry.

Museums and Cultural Centers

Museo Nacional de Arqueología y Etnología: Journey into Guatemala's Pre-Columbian Past

The Museo Nacional de Arqueología y Etnología is a captivating institution that takes visitors on a remarkable journey into Guatemala's pre-Columbian past. Located in Guatemala City, this museum is dedicated to preserving and showcasing the country's rich archaeological and ethnographic heritage. As you step inside, you will be greeted by a world of ancient civilizations, offering a glimpse into the lives and achievements of the Mayan people and other indigenous cultures.

The museum's exhibits feature a wide range of artifacts, including intricate pottery, stone carvings, jewelry, and textiles. These artifacts provide valuable insights into the artistic, religious, and daily life practices of Guatemala's ancient civilizations. The collection includes significant pieces from renowned archaeological sites such as Tikal, El Mirador, and Kaminaljuyu, allowing visitors to appreciate the depth and diversity of Guatemala's pre-Columbian history.

One of the highlights of the Museo Nacional de Arqueología y Etnología is its Maya Hall, which showcases a stunning array of Maya art and artifacts. Here, you can marvel at intricately carved stelae, examine exquisite ceramics, and learn about the hieroglyphic writing system that was developed by the Maya. The museum also provides comprehensive explanations and interactive displays to help visitors understand the cultural significance and historical context of each artifact.

In addition to the Maya Hall, the museum features sections dedicated to other indigenous cultures of Guatemala, such as the Olmec, Mam, and Quiché. These displays shed light on the diverse heritage of the country, highlighting the contributions of various ancient civilizations that inhabited the region long before the arrival of European settlers.

Visiting the Museo Nacional de Arqueología y Etnología is an opportunity to deepen your understanding of Guatemala's past and appreciate the ingenuity and cultural richness of its indigenous peoples. Whether you're an avid history enthusiast or simply curious about the origins of Guatemala's vibrant culture, this museum offers a captivating experience that will leave you in awe of the country's ancient civilizations.

Museo Popol Vuh: A Treasure Trove of Maya Art and Artifacts

Nestled within the grounds of the Universidad Francisco Marroquín in Guatemala City, the Museo Popol Vuh is a treasure trove of Maya art and artifacts. Named after the sacred Maya book, the Popol Vuh, this museum provides a captivating exploration of the ancient Maya civilization, showcasing their art, religious beliefs, and cultural traditions.

The Museo Popol Vuh boasts an extensive collection of Maya ceramics, sculptures, textiles, and jewelry. Each artifact tells a story, offering glimpses into the daily lives, rituals, and beliefs of the Maya people. The museum's exhibits are thoughtfully curated, taking visitors on a chronological journey through the different periods of Maya history, from the Preclassic to the Postclassic era.

One of the highlights of the Museo Popol Vuh is the collection of intricately crafted Maya ceramics. These vessels are adorned with intricate patterns and depict scenes from mythology, rituals, and everyday life. The attention to detail and artistic skill exhibited in these ceramics is truly remarkable, reflecting the Maya's deep connection to their natural surroundings and their spiritual beliefs.

The museum also showcases a remarkable collection of Maya textiles, known for their vibrant colors and intricate weaving techniques. These textiles offer a glimpse into the rich textile heritage of Guatemala and the significance of textiles in Maya society. From traditional clothing to ceremonial garments, the collection showcases the mastery of the Maya weavers and their ability to express their cultural identity through fabric.

Beyond the art and artifacts, the Museo Popol Vuh also delves into the religious and spiritual beliefs of the Maya civilization. Through interactive displays and multimedia presentations, visitors can gain insights into Maya cosmology, their intricate pantheon of gods and goddesses, and their religious rituals.

A visit to the Museo Popol Vuh is an immersive experience that allows visitors to appreciate the depth and complexity of Maya culture. The museum's commitment to education and preservation ensures that the legacy of the Maya civilization continues to inspire and enlighten future generations.

Museo Ixchel del Traje Indígena: Exploring Guatemala's Rich Textile Heritage

Located within the Universidad Francisco Marroquín, the Museo Ixchel del Traje Indígena is a cultural gem dedicated to exploring Guatemala's rich textile heritage. This museum is a testament to the artistry and craftsmanship of Guatemala's indigenous communities, showcasing the beauty and cultural significance of traditional clothing, known as "traje."

The Museo Ixchel del Traje Indígena houses an extensive collection of textiles, spanning different regions and ethnic groups of Guatemala. The exhibits highlight the intricate weaving techniques, vibrant colors, and symbolic motifs that are characteristic of each community's distinct style. Visitors have the opportunity to admire intricate huipiles (traditional blouses), cortes (skirts), and other garments, each representing a unique fusion of ancestral traditions and contemporary expressions.

The museum provides valuable insights into the cultural significance of textiles in Guatemala. Through interactive displays and educational materials, visitors can learn about the symbolism behind the patterns, colors, and weaving techniques. These textiles serve as a visual language, communicating aspects of identity, social status, and community belonging.

In addition to the textile collection, the Museo Ixchel del Traje Indígena offers workshops and demonstrations that allow visitors to witness the weaving process firsthand. You can observe skilled artisans as they transform raw fibers into intricate textiles, gaining a deeper appreciation for the time-honored techniques passed down through generations.

Furthermore, the museum collaborates with local communities to support the preservation of traditional weaving practices. By purchasing textiles directly from artisans, the Museo Ixchel del Traje Indígena contributes to the sustainability and economic empowerment of indigenous weavers.

A visit to the Museo Ixchel del Traje Indígena is a celebration of Guatemala's cultural diversity and a tribute to the ancestral knowledge and craftsmanship of its indigenous communities. It is a place where the beauty of textiles intertwines with the stories and traditions of the people who create them, offering a profound understanding of Guatemala's textile heritage.

Centro Cultural Miguel Ángel Asturias: A Hub for Arts and Performances

The Centro Cultural Miguel Ángel Asturias, named after the renowned Guatemalan writer and diplomat, is a vibrant hub for arts and performances in Guatemala City. This cultural center, also known as the Teatro Nacional, is a testament to

Guatemala's commitment to fostering creativity and preserving its cultural heritage.

The Centro Cultural Miguel Ángel Asturias is an architectural marvel, designed by the celebrated Guatemalan architect Efraín Recinos. Its distinctive modernist design incorporates elements inspired by Maya and colonial architecture, creating a visually striking and harmonious space. The center consists of multiple venues, including theaters, exhibition halls, and rehearsal studios, accommodating a wide range of artistic disciplines and events.

One of the highlights of the Centro Cultural Miguel Ángel Asturias is its theaters, which host a diverse program of performances throughout the year. From ballet and contemporary dance to theater productions, concerts, and opera, the center showcases both national and international talent, making it a cultural focal point for the city.

The center also serves as a platform for the preservation and promotion of traditional Guatemalan arts and folklore. Folkloric dance troupes and traditional music ensembles frequently grace the stages, offering audiences a glimpse into the country's rich cultural traditions. These performances celebrate Guatemala's multicultural heritage, showcasing the vibrant costumes, music, and dances of different indigenous communities.

In addition to live performances, the Centro Cultural Miguel Ángel Asturias hosts art exhibitions, film screenings, literary events, and educational workshops. The center's commitment to multidisciplinary arts and cultural exchange ensures that there is always something to engage and inspire visitors of all ages and interests.

A visit to the Centro Cultural Miguel Ángel Asturias is an invitation to immerse yourself in Guatemala's thriving artistic scene. Whether you are captivated by a theatrical performance, moved by a musical concert, or inspired by an art exhibition, this cultural center provides a platform for creativity, dialogue, and the celebration of Guatemala's rich artistic heritage.

Museo Miraflores: Unraveling the Ancient History of the Maya Civilization

Located in the outskirts of Guatemala City, the Museo Miraflores offers a captivating journey into the ancient history of the Maya civilization. This archaeological museum is situated atop the Miraflores hill, overlooking the city and providing visitors with a panoramic view while immersing them in the fascinating world of the Maya.

The Museo Miraflores focuses on the ancient city of Kaminaljuyu, one of the most significant Maya archaeological sites in the region. The museum's exhibits showcase the archaeological findings from Kaminaljuyu, including intricate pottery, stone carvings, jade jewelry, and architectural models. These artifacts offer valuable insights into the urban planning, religious practices, and daily life of the Maya people who inhabited Kaminaljuyu.

As visitors explore the museum, they can follow the chronological development of Kaminaljuyu, from its early beginnings as a farming village to its peak as a sophisticated urban center. The exhibits provide detailed information about the city's architecture, political organization, and economic activities, shedding light on the complexity and achievements of Maya civilization.

One of the standout features of the Museo Miraflores is the life-sized replica of a Maya tomb. Visitors can venture into the recreated tomb and witness the burial offerings and funerary rituals that were part of Maya beliefs and practices. This immersive experience provides a glimpse into the Maya's spiritual world and their views on the afterlife.

The Museo Miraflores also boasts an outdoor area that features reconstructed Maya structures, including a ballcourt and a pyramid. These structures offer visitors an opportunity to visualize how the ancient city would have looked and feel the presence of the past in a tangible way.

Moreover, the museum provides educational programs and workshops that engage visitors of all ages. Through hands-on activities and interactive displays, visitors can deepen their understanding of the Maya civilization and experience archaeology firsthand.

A visit to the Museo Miraflores is a captivating journey through time, unraveling the mysteries of the Maya civilization and fostering a deeper appreciation for their remarkable cultural and architectural achievements. It is an opportunity to connect with Guatemala's ancient past and gain a greater understanding of the profound impact the Maya have had on the region.

Museo del Ferrocarril: Tracing Guatemala's Railway Legacy

Situated in the heart of Guatemala City, the Museo del Ferrocarril offers a captivating exploration of the country's railway legacy. Housed within the historic "Estación Central," this museum provides a window into Guatemala's transportation history, tracing the development of its railway system and its impact on the nation's growth and cultural identity.

The Museo del Ferrocarril showcases a diverse collection of vintage locomotives, carriages, and railway artifacts. These artifacts reflect the evolution of Guatemala's railway technology and offer a glimpse into the golden age of rail travel. Visitors can marvel at the craftsmanship and engineering of the steam locomotives, admiring their elegant designs and intricate mechanisms.

The exhibits at the Museo del Ferrocarril provide a comprehensive overview of the railway's significance in Guatemala's economic and social development. Through photographs, maps, and historical documents, visitors can trace the routes of the railway lines and learn about their impact on trade, industry, and the movement of people within the country.

One of the highlights of the museum is the opportunity to step inside some of the vintage carriages and experience what train travel was like in the past. The meticulously restored interiors allow visitors to envision the bygone era of rail travel, with its plush seating, polished woodwork, and nostalgic ambiance.

Beyond the locomotives and carriages, the Museo del Ferrocarril offers insights into the daily lives of the railway workers. Exhibits dedicated to the employees showcase their uniforms, tools, and personal stories, shedding light on the human side of the railway industry and the dedication of those who kept the trains running.

Additionally, the museum organizes guided tours and educational activities for visitors of all ages. These programs provide a deeper understanding of the railway's historical context and its significance in shaping Guatemala's modern infrastructure.

A visit to the Museo del Ferrocarril is a journey through time, allowing visitors to appreciate the ingenuity of Guatemala's railway pioneers and gain a greater understanding of the country's transportation history. It is a testament to the enduring legacy of the railway and its role in shaping Guatemala's cultural heritage.

Gastronomy and Nightlife

Traditional Guatemalan Cuisine: From Street Food to Fine Dining

Guatemala's culinary scene is a reflection of its diverse cultural heritage, blending indigenous Mayan traditions with Spanish, African, and Caribbean influences. From street food stalls to upscale restaurants, Guatemala City offers a wide range of dining experiences that showcase the rich flavors and ingredients of Guatemalan cuisine.

The city is filled with food vendors and street food stalls that entice locals and visitors alike with their aromatic dishes. One of the most popular street foods is the "tortilla," a staple in Guatemalan cuisine. These thin, round corn or flour tortillas serve as the foundation for many dishes. You'll find street vendors skillfully preparing "tortillas" and serving them with a variety of fillings such as "revolcado" (spiced pork stew), "pepian" (a traditional Guatemalan stew), or "chuchitos" (steamed corn dumplings).

For those seeking a more refined dining experience, Guatemala City boasts a selection of fine dining establishments that elevate traditional Guatemalan flavors. These restaurants often focus on using locally sourced ingredients and incorporating traditional cooking techniques. One iconic dish is "fiambre," a cold salad traditionally prepared for the Day of the Dead celebrations. It is a colorful mix of meats, vegetables, cheeses, and pickled items, all dressed in a tangy vinaigrette. Other dishes that showcase the sophistication of Guatemalan cuisine include "jocon" (a savory chicken stew with green sauce), "pepian de pollo" (chicken in a rich, flavorful sauce), and "tapado" (a seafood soup made with coconut milk).

Exploring the Flavors of Guatemala: Typical Dishes and Ingredients

Guatemalan cuisine is characterized by the use of fresh, locally sourced ingredients that reflect the country's diverse ecosystems. The flavors are bold, often combining sweet, savory, and spicy elements to create a harmonious balance on the palate.

One of the essential ingredients in Guatemalan cuisine is corn. Corn is not only a dietary staple but also holds cultural and symbolic significance for the Mayan people. It is used to make tortillas, tamales, atol (a traditional hot corn beverage), and various snacks. The corn is often prepared through nixtamalization, a traditional process of soaking and cooking corn in an alkaline solution to improve its nutritional value and flavor.

Another prominent ingredient in Guatemalan cuisine is black beans. They are a versatile legume used in many traditional dishes, including "frijoles volteados" (refried black beans), which are typically served as a side dish with rice and tortillas. Beans are also a key component of "subanik" (a traditional Mayan dish made with black beans, chiles, and spices) and "pepián de pollo" (a chicken stew with a rich sauce made from ground pumpkin seeds and spices).

Guatemala's tropical climate lends itself to an abundance of fresh fruits and vegetables. Mangoes, avocados, papayas, pineapples, and bananas are widely available and used in both savory and sweet dishes. "Jocón" is a traditional chicken stew made with a vibrant green sauce that derives its color and flavor from ingredients like tomatillos, cilantro, green peppers, and spices.

To fully experience the flavors of Guatemala, a visit to the Mercado de Artesanías is a must. This bustling market offers an array of local delicacies and snacks. Here, you can sample traditional Guatemalan street food such as "elote loco" (grilled corn on the cob topped with mayonnaise, cheese, and spices), "tostadas" (crispy tortillas piled high with various toppings), and "empanadas" (fried turnovers filled with meats, cheeses, or vegetables). The market is also a great place to purchase local ingredients and spices to take home as culinary souvenirs.

Enjoying Guatemala City's Skyline Views: Rooftop Bars and Restaurants

Guatemala City's skyline is dotted with rooftop bars and restaurants that offer not only delectable cuisine but also breathtaking views of the cityscape. These elevated venues provide a unique dining experience where guests can savor their meals while enjoying panoramic vistas of the bustling city below.

Rooftop bars and restaurants in Guatemala City cater to a range of preferences, from casual hangouts to upscale establishments. Many of these venues feature stylish décor, comfortable seating, and trendy ambiance, creating a sophisticated setting for both locals and tourists to unwind and enjoy the city's vibrant atmosphere.

As you ascend to the rooftop, you'll be greeted by a diverse culinary scene that offers a fusion of international flavors and traditional Guatemalan dishes. Whether you're in the mood for a refreshing cocktail, a light bite, or a full-course meal, you'll find options to suit every palate.

Sip on a handcrafted cocktail while taking in the panoramic views of the city at sunset. Taste the flavors of Guatemala through innovative dishes that incorporate local ingredients and culinary techniques. From ceviche made with fresh seafood sourced from the nearby Pacific Coast to grilled meats and vegetables prepared with traditional spices and marinades, the rooftop dining experience in Guatemala City promises to be a feast for the senses.

Not only do these rooftop venues offer delicious food and stunning views, but they also serve as social hubs where locals and visitors gather to connect, celebrate, and enjoy memorable moments. Whether it's a romantic dinner, a lively gathering with friends, or a special occasion, rooftop bars and restaurants in Guatemala City provide a unique and unforgettable dining experience.

Mariscal District: Nightlife and Entertainment Hotspot

When the sun sets in Guatemala City, the Mariscal District comes alive with its vibrant nightlife and entertainment options. Located in Zone 10, this bustling neighborhood is known for its energetic atmosphere, lively bars, clubs, and diverse culinary offerings.

The Mariscal District caters to a variety of tastes and preferences, offering an eclectic mix of venues ranging from laid-back bars to energetic nightclubs. Whether you're in the mood for a relaxed evening sipping cocktails or dancing the night away, there's something for everyone.

The district's bars and pubs offer a laid-back ambiance, providing the perfect setting to socialize and unwind. Here, you can enjoy a wide selection of local and international beers, craft cocktails, and an extensive menu of bar snacks. The friendly and welcoming atmosphere makes it easy to strike up conversations with both locals and fellow travelers.

For those seeking a livelier experience, the Mariscal District is home to numerous nightclubs and music venues. Dance to the rhythm of Latin beats, reggaeton, electronic music, or enjoy live performances by local bands and DJs. The district's vibrant nightlife scene ensures that there is always something happening, whether it's themed parties, live music events, or cultural celebrations.

As you navigate the Mariscal District's streets, you'll also find an array of restaurants serving diverse cuisines from around the world. From traditional Guatemalan dishes to international flavors, the district offers a culinary journey for food enthusiasts. Indulge in mouthwatering dishes, sample creative cocktails, and experience the fusion of flavors that the district's restaurants have to offer.

Experiencing Guatemala's Vibrant Night Scene: Live Music and Cultural Performances

Guatemala City's vibrant night scene goes beyond bars and clubs; it also encompasses live music and cultural performances that showcase the country's rich artistic heritage. From traditional folk music to contemporary rhythms, the city offers a range of venues where you can immerse yourself in Guatemala's vibrant music and cultural scene.

Live music venues feature local bands, solo artists, and ensembles performing a variety of genres, including traditional Marimba music, salsa, cumbia, jazz, and rock. The infectious beats and lively performances create an energetic atmosphere that encourages dancing and celebration. Many of these venues also host cultural events and festivals, providing opportunities to experience the country's diverse artistic expressions.

In addition to live music, Guatemala City offers cultural performances that highlight traditional dances, theatrical productions, and storytelling. The National Theater hosts a variety of performances, including ballet, theater, and opera, showcasing both local and international talent. Cultural centers and museums also organize regular events, such as traditional dance performances and art exhibitions, providing a platform for artists to showcase their work and share their cultural heritage.

Attending a live music or cultural performance in Guatemala City is not only a chance to be entertained but also an opportunity to gain a deeper understanding of the country's history, traditions, and artistic expressions. It allows visitors to connect with the local culture and appreciate the talent and creativity of Guatemalan artists.

As the night unfolds in Guatemala City, the vibrant music and cultural scene come alive, offering a dynamic and engaging experience for both locals and visitors. Whether you choose to dance to the rhythms of traditional music, enjoy live performances, or simply soak up the energetic atmosphere, Guatemala City's nightlife and cultural scene will leave you with lasting memories of your visit.

In conclusion, Guatemala City's culinary scene, rooftop bars, nightlife hotspots, and vibrant music and cultural performances offer a diverse range of experiences for visitors. From sampling traditional Guatemalan cuisine and exploring the flavors of the local ingredients to enjoying skyline views while dining at rooftop establishments, the city provides a culinary adventure for food enthusiasts. The Mariscal District comes alive at night, offering a vibrant nightlife and entertainment scene, where visitors can socialize, dance, and enjoy live music performances. Guatemala City's cultural scene showcases the country's rich artistic heritage through traditional dances, theatrical performances, and live music, providing an immersive experience in Guatemala's vibrant cultural expressions. Whether you're a food lover, a nightlife enthusiast, or an art and music aficionado, Guatemala City's highlights will captivate your senses and leave you with a deep appreciation for the city's cultural and culinary offerings

La Aurora Zoo: Discovering Wildlife in the Heart of the City

Overview of La Aurora Zoo: Guatemala City's Premier Wildlife Park

La Aurora Zoo is undoubtedly one of the premier attractions in Guatemala City, offering visitors a unique opportunity to immerse themselves in the diverse and captivating world of wildlife. Nestled within the heart of the bustling capital, this expansive zoo is home to a wide array of exotic species from around the world. With its commitment to education, conservation, and family-friendly activities, La Aurora Zoo has become a beloved destination for locals and tourists alike.

Animal Encounters: Spotting Exotic Species from Around the World

At La Aurora Zoo, visitors can embark on a thrilling journey to encounter animals from various continents and ecosystems. The zoo boasts an impressive collection of species, ranging from native Central American creatures to representatives from Africa, Asia, and beyond. As you wander through the carefully designed habitats, you may come face-to-face with majestic big cats such as lions, tigers, and jaguars. The primates section is equally captivating, featuring playful monkeys, curious lemurs, and intelligent orangutans.

For those fascinated by reptiles, the herpetarium showcases an assortment of snakes, lizards, and turtles, including the venomous and elusive Fer-de-Lance snake. In the aviary, colorful tropical birds of all sizes fill the air with their melodic songs, while the aquatic exhibits introduce visitors to mesmerizing marine life, including vibrant fish and graceful sea turtles.

Educational Programs and Conservation Efforts

La Aurora Zoo is not just a place for entertainment; it also serves as an educational institution dedicated to raising awareness about the importance of wildlife conservation. The zoo offers a range of educational programs and interactive experiences designed to deepen visitors' understanding of animal behavior, ecosystems, and the challenges faced by endangered species.

Through guided tours and informative signage, visitors can learn about the conservation efforts carried out by the zoo to protect and preserve threatened species. They can also gain insight into the vital role zoos play in breeding programs and reintroduction initiatives aimed at ensuring the survival of endangered animals.

Botanical Gardens: Exploring the Flora of Guatemala

In addition to its remarkable collection of animals, La Aurora Zoo is also home to stunning botanical gardens that showcase the rich and diverse flora of Guatemala. As you stroll through the lush greenery, you'll encounter a vast variety of native plants, including vibrant orchids, exotic bromeliads, and towering ceiba trees. The botanical gardens provide a serene and picturesque setting, offering visitors a chance to connect with nature and appreciate the natural beauty of the region.

Family-Friendly Activities and Events

La Aurora Zoo is a perfect destination for families seeking a fun-filled day of exploration and discovery. The zoo offers a range of family-friendly activities and events designed to engage visitors of all ages. Children can participate in interactive workshops, educational games, and storytelling sessions that promote a deeper understanding and appreciation of wildlife.

One of the highlights for families is the opportunity to feed and interact with certain animals under the supervision of trained staff. These close encounters create lasting memories and allow visitors to develop a personal connection with the animal kingdom.

Throughout the year, La Aurora Zoo also hosts special events and exhibits that add an extra element of excitement to the zoo experience. From themed festivals and art exhibitions to conservation workshops and animal enrichment demonstrations, there is always something new and captivating happening at the zoo.

Conservation Initiatives and Community Involvement

La Aurora Zoo is not only committed to providing a memorable experience for its visitors but also actively engages in conservation initiatives and community involvement. The zoo collaborates with local and international organizations to support wildlife conservation efforts, including habitat preservation, breeding programs, and public awareness campaigns.

Moreover, La Aurora Zoo plays an integral role in the local community by offering educational opportunities to schools and hosting workshops that promote environmental stewardship. The zoo's commitment to sustainability is reflected in its green practices, such as waste management and energy conservation, ensuring that it operates in an environmentally responsible manner.

La Aurora Zoo stands as a testament to Guatemala City's dedication to wildlife conservation, education, and family entertainment. With its diverse collection of animals from around the world, engaging educational programs, beautiful botanical gardens, and family-friendly activities, the zoo offers an unforgettable experience for visitors of all ages. Whether you're an animal lover, nature enthusiast, or simply looking for a day of exploration, La Aurora Zoo is a must-visit destination that will leave you with a deeper appreciation for the wonders of the animal kingdom and the importance of conservation.

Plaza Barrios: Immerse in Local Culture and People-Watching

Plaza Barrios: A Central Gathering Spot in Guatemala City

Nestled in the heart of Guatemala City, Plaza Barrios is more than just a public square—it is a vibrant hub that pulsates with the energy of the city. As one of the most prominent gathering spots in the capital, it attracts both locals and visitors, creating a lively and diverse atmosphere. Named after the renowned Guatemalan poet, Justo Rufino Barrios, this historic plaza holds a significant place in the cultural and social life of the city.
Justo Rufino Barrios, after whom the plaza is named, was an influential figure in Guatemala's history. Born in 1835, Barrios rose to prominence as a political leader and reformer. He played a crucial role in modernizing the country during his presidency from 1873 to 1885. Barrios implemented numerous social and economic reforms, such as the expansion of education, the promotion of infrastructure development, and the abolition of indigenous communal landholdings. His visionary leadership and dedication to progress made him an iconic figure in Guatemala's history and earned him a place of honor at the heart of the city.

Plaza Barrios itself is steeped in history and has witnessed the transformation of Guatemala City over the years. Initially established during the Spanish colonial era, the plaza has evolved to reflect the changing times while preserving its historical significance. It has served as a focal point for political gatherings, public celebrations, and cultural events throughout the city's history.

Today, Plaza Barrios continues to be a beloved destination for locals and tourists alike, offering a myriad of experiences that showcase the essence of Guatemala. The bustling atmosphere is contagious, with the sound of laughter, music, and conversations filling the air. It is a place where people come together to connect, share stories, and celebrate the vibrant spirit of the city.

The diverse offerings at Plaza Barrios cater to various interests and tastes. Artisans and vendors set up stalls, displaying their crafts, jewelry, textiles, and other locally made products. This creates an opportunity for visitors to explore and support Guatemala's rich artistic traditions. The plaza's open spaces invite people to relax on benches, soak in the surroundings, and watch the ebb and flow of daily life.

Moreover, Plaza Barrios serves as a venue for community events and cultural festivals. Throughout the year, it comes alive with vibrant displays of music, dance, and theater. Local and international artists take the stage, showcasing their talents and celebrating the country's cultural heritage. From traditional dance performances to contemporary music concerts, the plaza offers a captivating lineup of entertainment that appeals to a wide audience.

The plaza is also an ideal spot for people of all ages to engage in leisurely activities. Families gather for picnics, children play games, and friends meet for a leisurely chat. The open spaces provide a sense of freedom and camaraderie, fostering connections and strengthening the social fabric of the community.

Surrounding the plaza, visitors will discover the architectural gems that reflect Guatemala's history and blend with modern elements. Historical buildings with colonial facades stand alongside modern structures, creating a visual tapestry that tells the story of Guatemala's past and present.

Plaza Barrios is not only a physical space; it is a symbol of the city's resilience, creativity, and the strong sense of identity that defines Guatemala. It represents the convergence of history, art, culture, and community. Whether you're strolling through the plaza, enjoying the performances, or simply people-watching, Plaza Barrios provides an immersive experience that allows you to connect with the vibrant soul of Guatemala City. It encapsulates the essence of the city—a dynamic, diverse, and welcoming place where traditions thrive and new stories unfold every day.

Local Vendors and Street Food: Sampling Guatemalan Delights

One of the highlights of Plaza Barrios is the array of local vendors and street food stalls that line its pathways. As you stroll through the square, you'll be enticed by the tantalizing aromas of Guatemalan cuisine. The air is filled with the scent of sizzling meats, freshly baked tortillas, and a medley of spices. From the iconic tamales and chuchitos (Guatemalan tamales) to the mouthwatering pupusas (stuffed tortillas) and empanadas, Plaza Barrios offers a gastronomic adventure that will delight your taste buds.

Sampling Guatemalan street food is not just about indulging in delicious flavors; it's also a window into the country's culinary traditions and cultural heritage. Vendors proudly showcase their regional specialties, using age-old recipes passed down through generations. Each dish tells a story, reflecting the diverse influences of Mayan, Spanish, and

African cultures that have shaped Guatemala's culinary landscape.

Cultural Performances and Entertainment

Plaza Barrios is not only a place to satisfy your appetite but also a hub of cultural performances and entertainment. The square comes alive with vibrant displays of traditional music, dance, and theater, showcasing Guatemala's rich artistic heritage. Local musicians fill the air with melodies played on traditional instruments such as marimbas, guitars, and drums, creating a lively and captivating atmosphere.

Visitors to Plaza Barrios can witness traditional dance performances that pay homage to Guatemala's indigenous roots. Colorful costumes, intricate choreography, and rhythmic movements bring ancient Mayan traditions to life. These performances not only entertain but also preserve and celebrate Guatemala's cultural identity.

Cultural festivals and events are also held at Plaza Barrios throughout the year. From the vibrant Independence Day celebrations to the solemn Holy Week processions, the plaza becomes a focal point for communal gatherings and shared experiences. These festivities provide an opportunity for both locals and tourists to engage with Guatemala's cultural tapestry and create lasting memories.

Traditional Games and Activities for All Ages

Plaza Barrios is a place where people of all ages can come together and engage in traditional games and activities. Families gather to enjoy quality time while participating in recreational pursuits that have been part of Guatemalan culture for generations. Children can be seen flying kites high in the sky, their colorful creations adding a touch of whimsy to the plaza.

In addition to kite-flying, traditional games such as sack races, marbles, and spinning tops are enjoyed by both young and old. These activities foster a sense of camaraderie and playfulness, as laughter fills the air and bonds are formed between generations. Plaza Barrios provides a space where the old and the new seamlessly blend, where modern technology takes a backseat to the timeless joys of simple, traditional games.

Historical Monuments and Sculptures

As you explore Plaza Barrios, you'll encounter several historical monuments and sculptures that pay tribute to significant figures and events in Guatemalan history. These landmarks serve as a reminder of the country's rich past and the struggles and triumphs that have shaped its identity.

One notable monument is the statue of Justo Rufino Barrios, after whom the plaza is named. Barrios was a prominent statesman and reformer who played a pivotal role in Guatemala's modernization during the late 19th century. The monument stands tall, commemorating his contributions to the nation's progress.

Another prominent feature is the Monumento a la Revolución, a striking sculpture dedicated to the memory of the Guatemalan Revolution of 1944. The monument symbolizes the country's fight for democracy and social justice, reminding visitors of the transformative moments in Guatemala's history.

Plaza Barrios serves as a platform for these historical monuments and sculptures, providing a public space where locals and tourists can reflect upon and appreciate the legacy of their ancestors. It's a place where history comes alive, bridging the gap between the past and the present.

In conclusion, Plaza Barrios in Guatemala City offers a captivating blend of cultural experiences, culinary delights, entertainment, and historical significance. This central gathering spot embodies the vibrant spirit of Guatemala, inviting visitors to immerse themselves in the country's traditions, flavors, and stories. Whether you're savoring the delectable street food, witnessing captivating cultural performances, engaging in traditional games, or contemplating the historical monuments, Plaza Barrios provides a truly immersive and memorable experience that reflects the essence of Guatemala's capital city.

La Bodeguita del Centro: A Culinary Adventure through Guatemala's Tastes

La Bodeguita del Centro: Gastronomic Hub of Guatemala City

Located in the heart of Guatemala City, La Bodeguita del Centro stands as a vibrant gastronomic hub, enticing locals and tourists alike with its rich culinary offerings. This bustling marketplace captures the essence of Guatemala's diverse regional cuisine, showcasing an array of flavors, ingredients, and cooking techniques that have shaped the country's culinary identity. With its lively atmosphere and tempting aromas, La Bodeguita del Centro invites visitors on a mouthwatering journey through Guatemala's gastronomic landscape.

Regional Cuisine: Tasting Flavors from Different Parts of Guatemala

La Bodeguita del Centro is a culinary paradise that celebrates the diverse regional cuisines of Guatemala. Each region in the country boasts its own unique flavors and traditional dishes, influenced by indigenous Mayan heritage, Spanish colonialism, and other cultural influences. From the hearty stews of the highlands to the seafood delicacies of the coastal regions, visitors can savor the distinct tastes that define each area.

In the market's stalls and food stands, visitors can sample dishes such as pepián, a flavorful meat stew with a rich sauce made from roasted seeds and spices, which originated in the Mayan highlands. The coastal regions offer delectable seafood options, including ceviche, a refreshing dish of marinated raw fish or shrimp, bursting with citrus flavors and vibrant colors. Those looking for a vegetarian delight can try chiles rellenos, a dish consisting of stuffed peppers filled with cheese, vegetables, or meat, accompanied by a flavorful tomato sauce.

Culinary Workshops and Cooking Classes

For those eager to delve deeper into Guatemala's culinary heritage, La Bodeguita del Centro offers culinary workshops and cooking classes. These hands-on experiences provide participants with the opportunity to learn traditional cooking techniques and prepare authentic Guatemalan dishes under the guidance of expert chefs.

During these workshops, participants can gain insights into the unique ingredients and spices used in Guatemalan cuisine. They can learn the art of making tortillas from scratch, a staple food in Guatemala, and explore the secrets of preparing traditional salsas and sauces that complement the country's dishes. These interactive sessions not only provide a chance to learn new recipes but also offer a deeper appreciation for the cultural significance of Guatemalan cuisine.

Artisanal Beverages and Traditional Drinks

No culinary journey through Guatemala is complete without exploring the country's diverse selection of artisanal beverages and traditional drinks. At La Bodeguita del Centro, visitors can quench their thirst with a variety of refreshing and flavorful options.

One popular traditional drink is atol, a warm and comforting beverage made from corn masa (dough) mixed with spices, such as cinnamon and vanilla. This traditional Mayan drink is often enjoyed alongside breakfast or as an afternoon pick-me-up. Another beloved beverage is horchata, a creamy and sweet rice-based drink flavored with cinnamon and often served over ice. Horchata is a delightful refreshment that perfectly complements the flavors of Guatemalan cuisine.

For those seeking a caffeine fix, Guatemala is renowned for its high-quality coffee. Visitors can sample different varieties of locally sourced coffee, from rich and robust espresso to smooth and aromatic pour-over brews. Coffee enthusiasts can even learn about the coffee production process, from the cultivation of the beans to the art of brewing a perfect cup, through educational workshops and tastings offered at La Bodeguita del Centro.

Food Tours and Tastings in La Bodeguita del Centro Market

To fully immerse oneself in the culinary delights of La Bodeguita del Centro, food tours and tastings are a must-do experience. Guided by local experts, these tours take visitors on a culinary adventure, allowing them to explore the market's vibrant stalls, interact with local vendors, and sample an array of mouthwatering dishes.

During the food tours, participants can learn about the history and cultural significance of the ingredients and dishes they encounter. They can engage with passionate food artisans who share their stories and knowledge, providing valuable insights into the traditions and techniques passed down through generations. From street food classics like tamales and pupusas to lesser-known delicacies waiting to be discovered, the food tours offer a delightful feast for the senses.

The market's tastings provide an opportunity to indulge in a curated selection of dishes and beverages. Visitors can savor the flavors of traditional Guatemalan street food, such as garnachas (fried tortillas topped with meat, cheese, and salsa) or chuchitos (steamed corn dumplings filled with meat or cheese). They can also sample artisanal cheeses, freshly baked bread, and exotic fruits sourced from different regions of Guatemala. With each bite and sip, the richness and diversity of Guatemalan cuisine come alive.

In conclusion, La Bodeguita del Centro serves as a gateway to the captivating world of Guatemalan gastronomy. It offers visitors a chance to experience the country's regional cuisine, partake in culinary workshops, and immerse themselves in the vibrant atmosphere of the market. With its diverse range of flavors, culinary traditions, and artisanal beverages, La Bodeguita del Centro beckons food enthusiasts to embark on a remarkable culinary journey through the heart of Guatemala City. Whether it's tasting traditional dishes, learning new cooking techniques, or simply enjoying the vibrant ambiance, this gastronomic hub is a must-visit for anyone seeking to explore the rich culinary heritage of Guatemala.

Chapter 4: Antigua Guatemala: Colonial Charms and Beyond

The UNESCO World Heritage Site

Antigua Guatemala, often referred to simply as Antigua, is a city that captivates visitors with its timeless beauty and historical significance. Nestled amidst a breathtaking landscape of picturesque volcanoes, this enchanting destination transports travelers back in time to the colonial era. Recognized as a UNESCO World Heritage Site, Antigua boasts exceptionally preserved architecture that showcases its rich history and cultural heritage.

As visitors step foot in Antigua, they are immediately greeted by the city's undeniable charm. The cobblestone streets, lined with vibrant facades and intricate architectural details, create a whimsical atmosphere reminiscent of a bygone era. The city's architectural splendor can be traced back to its colonial past, when it served as the capital of the Captaincy General of Guatemala, a region that spanned much of Central America. The remnants of this illustrious history can be witnessed through the magnificent churches, monasteries, and palaces that grace Antigua's landscape.

Wandering through the streets of Antigua is like stepping into a living museum of Spanish Baroque and Mudejar architecture. The facades of the buildings are adorned with decorative elements such as intricately carved stone reliefs, wrought iron balconies, and wooden doors with ornate carvings. Each step reveals a new architectural gem, showcasing the grandeur and artistry of the colonial period. Some notable examples include the iconic Cathedral of San José, the majestic La Merced Church, and the awe-inspiring Santa Catalina Arch.

The Cathedral of San José, located in the main square known as Parque Central, is a symbol of religious devotion and architectural excellence. Its vibrant yellow facade stands in stark contrast to the surrounding buildings, drawing the eyes of passersby. Step inside to behold its opulent interior, adorned with exquisite altarpieces, religious artwork, and intricately carved wooden choir stalls. The cathedral's sheer magnitude and artistic beauty are a testament to the city's rich religious heritage.

Another architectural masterpiece is the Church of La Merced, renowned for its stunning baroque facade. The intricate relief work and the combination of volcanic stone and stucco make it a visual feast for visitors. Step through its doors to discover a sanctuary filled with gilded altars, intricate frescoes, and a serene courtyard adorned with a central fountain. As you explore the church, you can't help but be in awe of the craftsmanship and devotion that went into creating this architectural gem.

While exploring Antigua, make sure to marvel at the Santa Catalina Arch, one of the city's most iconic landmarks. This archway, originally built to provide cloistered nuns a way to cross the street without being seen, now frames a breathtaking view of the surrounding volcanoes. The arch serves as a symbol of Antigua's rich history and offers a perfect photo opportunity that encapsulates the city's colonial charm.

Beyond its architectural wonders, Antigua Guatemala offers a vibrant cultural scene that celebrates its traditions and artistic expressions. The city is home to numerous art galleries and craft markets where visitors can immerse themselves in the local arts and crafts scene. The Mercado de Artesanías, located near the Central Park, is a treasure trove of handcrafted goods, ranging from intricate textiles and ceramics to vibrant paintings and jewelry. Exploring the market provides a glimpse into the skilled craftsmanship and indigenous traditions that are woven into the fabric of Guatemalan culture.

For a deeper understanding of Guatemala's indigenous textiles, a visit to the Museo Casa del Tejido Antiguo is a must. This museum showcases a remarkable collection of traditional textiles, showcasing various weaving techniques, patterns, and symbols that reflect the diverse indigenous cultures of Guatemala. Visitors can learn about the history and cultural significance of these textiles, engage with skilled weavers, and even participate in weaving workshops to gain hands-on experience in this ancient art form.

In addition to its cultural offerings, Antigua is also a hub for culinary delights. The city's culinary scene is a fusion of traditional Guatemalan flavors and international influences. Numerous restaurants and cafes offer a diverse range of dishes that cater to every palate. From traditional Guatemalan specialties like Pepián, a hearty meat stew, and Kak'ik, a spicy turkey soup, to international cuisines, Antigua's dining options are sure to satisfy even the most discerning food lovers.

Antigua's charm extends beyond its city limits, offering a wealth of outdoor activities and natural beauty to explore. The surrounding volcanoes provide a stunning backdrop for adventure seekers. Hiking enthusiasts can embark on exhilarating treks up Volcán de Agua, Volcán de Fuego, or even the challenging Volcán Acatenango. These hikes reward visitors with panoramic views of the lush landscapes, sprawling coffee plantations, and, if lucky, even the sight of molten lava from Volcán de Fuego.

For those seeking a more relaxed outdoor experience, Antigua offers opportunities for leisurely walks and bicycle rides. The outskirts of the city boast picturesque scenery, including rolling hills, verdant valleys, and coffee farms. Exploring these areas allows visitors to connect with nature, breathe in the fresh air, and admire the beauty that surrounds Antigua.

As you venture beyond the city, a visit to nearby villages provides a deeper understanding of the local culture and traditions. One such village is San Juan del Obispo, located just a short distance from Antigua. This quaint village is known for its pottery workshops, where visitors can witness skilled artisans mold clay into intricate vessels and decorative pieces. It is an opportunity to learn about the ancient techniques that have been passed down through generations and appreciate the craftsmanship involved in creating these beautiful works of art.

Ciudad Vieja, another nearby village, offers a glimpse into the historical roots of Guatemala. This village was once the original capital of the country before it was destroyed by a devastating earthquake in 1773. The ruins of Ciudad Vieja provide a fascinating insight into the country's past, with its remnants of churches, convents, and cobblestone streets. Exploring the village allows visitors to step back in time and imagine what life was like during the colonial era.

Exploring Antigua's Architecture and Churches

Antigua Guatemala, with its well-preserved colonial architecture, is a treasure trove of magnificent churches that offer a glimpse into the city's religious heritage. These architectural marvels stand as testaments to the rich history and cultural significance of Antigua. Among the notable churches in the city, the Cathedral of San José holds a prominent place.

Situated in the main square, Parque Central, the Cathedral of San José is an imposing structure that dates back to the 16th century. As you approach the cathedral, you'll be captivated by its striking yellow façade and intricate stonework, showcasing the craftsmanship of the era. Step inside to immerse yourself in the solemn atmosphere and appreciate the grandeur of the cathedral. The interior reveals a captivating blend of religious artifacts, delicate artwork, and a remarkable altar that has withstood the test of time. The cathedral's interior design is a testament to the devotion and artistic talent of the craftsmen who contributed to its construction.

Another must-visit church in Antigua is La Merced, renowned for its stunning baroque-style façade adorned with intricate relief work. The church stands as a testament to the architectural brilliance of the colonial era. As you step through the doors of La Merced, you'll be greeted by an awe-inspiring interior. The gilded altars, ornate carvings, and exquisite artwork create a sense of reverence and awe. Exploring further, you'll discover a serene courtyard with a central fountain, offering a tranquil oasis amidst the bustling city. Don't miss the opportunity to climb to the top of La Merced's bell tower, where you'll be rewarded with breathtaking panoramic views of Antigua's enchanting streetscape and the majestic surrounding volcanoes.

In addition to the Cathedral of San José and La Merced, Antigua boasts numerous other architectural gems that add to its allure. The Santa Catalina Arch stands as an iconic symbol of the city and serves as a lasting reminder of Antigua's colonial heritage. This arch frames the view of the magnificent Volcán de Agua, providing a picturesque backdrop for unforgettable photographs and capturing the essence of Antigua's unique charm.

The Palace of the Captains General, now serving as the City Hall, is another architectural gem worth exploring. This historic building showcases a fusion of architectural styles, blending Spanish colonial and Baroque influences. It stands as a testament to the city's administrative and political past. Within the Palace, the Museum of Santiago offers visitors the opportunity to delve into the history of Antigua and learn about the significant events and figures that shaped the city's development.

For those seeking a peaceful retreat from the bustling streets, the Convent of Santa Clara offers a serene sanctuary. Step into the tranquil courtyards adorned with lush gardens and ornate fountains, and feel a sense of tranquility wash over you. The convent houses a collection of religious artifacts, offering a glimpse into the spiritual practices and traditions of the past. Take a moment to appreciate the quietude and reflect on the historical significance of this sacred space.

As you explore the churches and architectural wonders of Antigua, you'll find yourself transported back in time, marveling at the craftsmanship and the devotion that went into creating these sacred spaces. Each church has its own unique story to tell, weaving together the tapestry of Antigua's religious and cultural heritage. Whether you're an architecture enthusiast, a history buff, or a seeker of spiritual inspiration, the churches of Antigua are sure to leave an indelible impression on your journey through this enchanting city.

Experiencing Antigua's Markets and Cuisine

A visit to Antigua Guatemala is a treat for food enthusiasts and those seeking a culinary adventure. The city's vibrant markets and diverse culinary scene offer a delightful fusion of flavors, aromas, and cultural experiences. Embark on a gastronomic journey and explore the local markets, savor traditional dishes, and even immerse yourself in a cooking class to learn the secrets of Guatemalan cuisine.

Start your culinary exploration in Antigua by visiting the local markets, where an array of sights, sounds, and smells will captivate your senses. The Mercado de Artesanías, located near the Central Park, is a bustling marketplace where vendors display a wide selection of handicrafts, textiles, and souvenirs. Explore the vibrant stalls, interact with the local artisans, and discover unique treasures that represent Guatemala's vibrant culture. From intricately woven textiles to handcrafted ceramics and vibrant paintings, the market offers a chance to bring home a piece of Antigua's artistic heritage.

While at the markets, be sure to sample the delicious street food and traditional Guatemalan snacks. The air is filled with tempting aromas of freshly prepared delicacies. One must-try dish is Pepián, a hearty meat stew with rich flavors that reflects the country's culinary heritage. This dish is often prepared with chicken or beef, simmered with a blend of aromatic spices, chilies, and vegetables, resulting in a deliciously complex and satisfying meal. Another culinary gem is Kak'ik, a spicy turkey soup infused with traditional Mayan spices. This flavorful soup is a perfect blend of earthy and aromatic flavors, showcasing the indigenous influences on Guatemalan cuisine.

To delve even deeper into the world of Guatemalan gastronomy, consider taking a cooking class. Antigua offers a range of immersive culinary experiences where you can learn to prepare traditional dishes under the guidance of local chefs. These classes provide a hands-on approach to understanding the ingredients, techniques, and cultural significance behind Guatemalan cuisine.

Master the art of making tortillas, a staple in Guatemalan cuisine, by grinding corn and shaping the dough into perfect circles. Explore the traditional methods of making Guatemalan salsas and sauces, which add vibrant flavors to dishes. Discover the importance of native ingredients like chilies, herbs, and spices that bring depth and complexity to Guatemalan recipes.

During the cooking classes, you'll have the opportunity to learn about the historical influences that have shaped Guatemalan flavors. From Mayan traditions to Spanish colonial influences, each dish tells a story of cultural fusion and culinary evolution. Gain insight into the significance of specific ingredients and how they have been used throughout Guatemala's rich history.

These immersive cooking experiences not only allow you to expand your culinary skills but also provide a cultural exchange as you interact with local chefs and fellow food enthusiasts. It's a chance to forge connections, learn from each other, and gain a deeper appreciation for the culinary heritage of Guatemala.

After the cooking class, sit down to enjoy the fruits of your labor and savor the authentic flavors of Guatemalan cuisine. Share the meal with newfound friends and engage in conversations about food, culture, and travel experiences. It's a rewarding and enriching experience that will leave you with lasting memories.

Outdoor Activities and Surrounding Villages

Beyond its architectural wonders and culinary delights, Antigua Guatemala is a gateway to a world of natural beauty and captivating villages that beckon to be explored. The region surrounding Antigua is blessed with a stunning backdrop of majestic volcanoes, including Volcán de Agua, Volcán de Fuego, and Volcán Acatenango. For adventurous travelers seeking unforgettable experiences, the opportunity to embark on volcano hikes awaits, offering the chance to witness breathtaking sunrises and even the awe-inspiring spectacle of fiery lava eruptions from Volcán de Fuego.

For those seeking a more relaxed outdoor experience, Antigua's outskirts offer a tranquil escape into picturesque landscapes, lush gardens, and verdant coffee plantations. Take a leisurely walk or hop on a bicycle to explore the surrounding areas, where every corner unveils a postcard-worthy view. As you venture through the countryside, you'll be greeted by the sweet aroma of coffee wafting through the air, as coffee plantations thrive in the fertile soil of this region. Consider a visit to a local coffee farm to learn about the cultivation and production processes, and savor a cup of freshly brewed coffee while soaking in the serene ambiance.

One notable destination that offers a tranquil retreat is the Earth Lodge, nestled on the slopes of Volcán de Agua. This eco-friendly lodge not only provides stunning panoramic views of the surrounding landscape but also offers unique accommodation options that blend harmoniously with nature. From cozy cabins to treehouses perched amidst the trees, the Earth Lodge allows you to disconnect from the hustle and bustle of everyday life and immerse yourself in the serene beauty of the Guatemalan countryside. Engage in yoga and meditation sessions, rejuvenate with holistic therapies, or simply unwind in the embrace of nature.

As you venture beyond Antigua, nearby villages beckon, each offering a glimpse into the rich local culture and traditions. One such village is San Juan del Obispo, located just a short distance from Antigua. This charming village exudes a tranquil ambiance and is known for its vibrant pottery workshops. Take a stroll through its cobblestone streets lined with colorful houses and visit the local artisans who have honed their pottery-making skills for generations. Observe their techniques as they shape clay into intricate designs, creating beautiful pottery that serves as a testament to Guatemala's artistic heritage.

Another village worth exploring is Ciudad Vieja, which holds historical significance as the original capital of Guatemala. Visit the ruins of Ciudad Vieja and step back in time as you wander through narrow streets lined with colonial-era churches and buildings. The ruins bear witness to the devastating effects of earthquakes that led to the city's relocation to its current site, Antigua. Explore the remnants of this once-flourishing city and imagine the grandeur it once possessed, providing insight into Guatemala's captivating past.

Immersing yourself in the daily lives of the locals is an enriching experience that allows you to connect with the heart and soul of Guatemala. Engage in conversations with the friendly villagers, learn about their customs, and witness their artistic talents. Whether it's witnessing a pottery-making demonstration, participating in a traditional weaving workshop, or savoring authentic local cuisine, these encounters offer a genuine glimpse into the traditions and way of life that have been passed down through generations.

In conclusion, Antigua Guatemala offers much more than its architectural wonders and culinary delights. The region surrounding Antigua presents a natural playground with awe-inspiring volcanoes and breathtaking landscapes waiting to be explored. Whether you choose to embark on volcano hikes to witness nature's raw power, take leisurely walks through coffee plantations, or find tranquility at eco-friendly lodges, the outdoor experiences are bound to leave a lasting impression. Additionally, the neighboring villages, such as San Juan del Obispo and Ciudad Vieja, provide an opportunity to delve deeper into local culture, interact with artisans, and gain a deeper appreciation for Guatemala's artistic and historical heritage. Antigua's allure extends far beyond its city limits, inviting you to uncover the treasures that lie just beyond its doorstep.

Antigua's Semana Santa: Witnessing a Spectacular Holy Week Celebration

Antigua Guatemala is internationally renowned for its breathtaking Semana Santa, a week-long celebration leading up to Easter Sunday. This religious festival is a time when the city comes alive with profound devotion, elaborate processions, and stunning displays of artistry. Semana Santa in Antigua is a unique and awe-inspiring experience that attracts both locals and visitors from around the world.

During Semana Santa, the streets of Antigua transform into a living canvas of religious fervor and artistic expression. One of the most captivating elements of the celebration is the creation of intricate alfombras, or carpets, which adorn the processional routes. These alfombras are meticulously crafted by hand using various natural materials, such as flower petals, colored sawdust, pine needles, and even fruits and vegetables. Skilled artisans and dedicated community members spend hours delicately arranging these materials to form intricate patterns, religious symbols, and scenes from the Bible.

Witnessing the creation of these ephemeral masterpieces is a truly mesmerizing experience. As you walk through the streets of Antigua in the days leading up to Easter, you'll encounter groups of people meticulously laying down the materials to create the alfombras. The atmosphere is filled with a sense of focus, creativity, and community as individuals work together, kneeling on the ground and carefully arranging each element. The result is a stunning display of colors and designs that stretch for blocks, enhancing the already beautiful colonial streets of Antigua.

The culmination of the Semana Santa celebrations are the processions that wind their way through the city's cobblestone streets. These processions are a sight to behold, with massive floats, known as andas, carried by a large group of men dressed in purple robes, known as cucuruchos. The andas are ornate structures adorned with religious statues and decorations, often weighing several tons. It is a testament to the strength, dedication, and devotion of the men who bear the weight of these sacred symbols on their shoulders.

Accompanying the andas are women dressed in black, known as las mujeres de luto, or the mourning women. They walk solemnly behind the floats, displaying their grief and solidarity with the suffering of Christ. The contrast of the vibrant purple robes and the mourning attire of the women creates a visually striking scene that adds to the intensity and emotional impact of the processions.

The processions are accompanied by hauntingly beautiful music played by bands, further heightening the atmosphere of reverence and solemnity. The melodies of brass instruments and drums echo through the streets, creating a hauntingly atmospheric backdrop to the religious spectacle. The music adds an emotional depth and a sense of spirituality that resonates with both participants and spectators.

As the processions make their way through the streets, crowds of onlookers gather to witness this grand display of faith and cultural heritage. Locals and visitors alike line the streets, filled with a sense of awe and respect for the traditions that have been passed down through generations. It is a time of deep religious reflection, as well as a celebration of Guatemalan culture and tradition.

Semana Santa in Antigua is a truly immersive experience that allows you to witness the devotion and artistic expressions of the local community. It is a time when the boundaries between the sacred and the secular blur, and the city becomes a stage for both religious rituals and cultural performances. The combination of intricate alfombras, massive andas, mournful women, and evocative music creates a sensory journey that leaves a lasting impression on all who participate.

Museums and Art Galleries: Exploring Antigua's Cultural Heritage

Antigua's vibrant cultural scene is not only reflected in its architecture and religious celebrations but also in its array of museums and art galleries. These cultural institutions serve as gateways to Guatemala's history, art, and indigenous traditions, providing visitors with a deeper understanding of the country's rich cultural heritage.

The Museo Casa del Tejido Antiguo (Museum of Ancient Weaving) is a must-visit destination for those fascinated by the art of traditional Guatemalan textiles. Located within a beautifully restored colonial-era building, the museum showcases a stunning collection of intricate weavings, each telling a story of Guatemala's indigenous cultures. As you step inside, you are greeted by a kaleidoscope of colors and patterns, ranging from vibrant huipiles (traditional blouses) to intricately woven rugs, tablecloths, and other textiles.

The exhibits in the museum highlight the diversity of weaving techniques, patterns, and motifs used by different indigenous groups throughout Guatemala. You can admire the masterful craftsmanship and learn about the symbolism behind each textile. The museum also offers interactive displays and demonstrations, allowing visitors to gain firsthand insights into the art of weaving. Skilled artisans are often present, working on their looms, and they are more than willing to share their knowledge and techniques with curious visitors.

For those seeking a deeper immersion in the world of art, Antigua is home to numerous art galleries that showcase a wide range of artistic styles and mediums. Galería El Túnel is a popular destination for art enthusiasts, featuring works by both local and international artists. The gallery exhibits a diverse collection of artwork, ranging from contemporary pieces that explore social and political issues to traditional art forms that pay homage to Guatemala's cultural heritage.

As you stroll through the gallery, you'll encounter vibrant paintings that depict the daily lives of Guatemalan people, sculptures that capture the essence of Mayan mythology, mesmerizing photographs that document the country's landscapes, and thought-provoking mixed media installations. Galería El Túnel serves as a platform for both established and emerging artists, fostering a vibrant artistic community and providing a space for creativity to flourish.

Delving further into Guatemala's history and archaeology, the Museo del Jade (Jade Museum) offers a captivating journey through the ancient civilizations that once thrived in the region. Jade holds immense cultural and spiritual significance in Mayan culture, and this museum houses an impressive collection of jade artifacts that provide insights into the Maya's reverence for this precious stone.

As you explore the museum, you'll encounter intricately carved jade masks, pendants, figurines, and other objects that showcase the extraordinary craftsmanship of the Mayan artisans. Each piece tells a story, representing various aspects of Maya mythology, rituals, and daily life. The museum not only highlights the aesthetic beauty of jade but also delves into its cultural significance, connecting visitors to Guatemala's ancient past and the enduring legacy of the Maya civilization.

By visiting these museums and art galleries in Antigua, visitors have the opportunity to immerse themselves in Guatemala's rich cultural heritage. They provide windows into the country's history, traditions, and artistic expressions, allowing visitors to appreciate the diverse tapestry that has shaped Guatemala's identity. Whether you find yourself marveling at the intricate weavings in the Museo Casa del Tejido Antiguo, exploring the eclectic artworks in Galería El Túnel, or delving into the ancient world of the Maya in the Museo del Jade, these cultural institutions offer unforgettable experiences that foster a deeper connection with Guatemala's vibrant culture.

In conclusion, Antigua Guatemala offers a captivating blend of colonial charm, architectural marvels, culinary delights, and outdoor adventures. With its UNESCO World Heritage status, the city stands as a testament to Guatemala's rich history and cultural heritage. Whether you're exploring the awe-inspiring churches and architectural landmarks, immersing yourself in the vibrant markets and culinary experiences, or venturing into the surrounding villages and natural landscapes, Antigua is sure to leave a lasting impression on every traveler fortunate enough to experience its wonders.

Chapter 5: Lake Atitlán and the Surrounding Villages

Lake Atitlán, often referred to as the "Pearl of Guatemala," is a stunningly beautiful volcanic lake nestled in the highlands of Guatemala. Surrounded by towering mountains and vibrant indigenous villages, Lake Atitlán offers a captivating experience for travelers seeking natural beauty, cultural immersion, and outdoor adventures.

Discovering the Enchanting Lake Atitlán

As you arrive at Lake Atitlán, you'll be greeted by a sight of awe-inspiring beauty that will leave an indelible mark on your memory. The first glimpse of the shimmering blue waters, framed by three majestic volcanoes—San Pedro, Atitlán, and Tolimán—creates a breathtaking panorama that seems almost too picturesque to be real. The sheer grandeur of the scene immediately captivates your senses, as if welcoming you into a world where nature's magnificence knows no bounds.

One of the best ways to fully immerse yourself in the splendor of Lake Atitlán is by taking a boat tour or renting a kayak to explore its pristine waters. The gentle waves lap against the sides of the vessel as you embark on a journey that promises both serenity and adventure. Gliding along the lake's surface, you become a spectator to the ever-changing landscape that unfolds before your eyes.

As you navigate the crystal-clear waters, you'll find yourself surrounded by a tapestry of natural wonders. The lake stretches out before you, revealing its vast expanse and inviting you to delve deeper into its secrets. The calmness of the water mirrors the tranquility of the surrounding environment, creating a sense of harmony that is both soothing and invigorating.

The picturesque landscapes that embrace Lake Atitlán are a testament to Mother Nature's artistry. Lush green hills cascade down to meet the water's edge, forming a verdant backdrop that accentuates the lake's radiant beauty. The vibrant hues of the flora that embellish the shoreline add a touch of brilliance to the scene, creating a feast for the eyes at every turn. It is as if the colors themselves have come alive, dancing harmoniously in celebration of nature's masterpiece.

As you venture farther into the heart of the lake, you'll discover hidden gems that dot its surface. Tiny islets emerge, seemingly suspended in time, each with its own story to tell. Some of these islands are inhabited, offering a glimpse into the daily lives of the locals who call Lake Atitlán home. Their humble dwellings blend seamlessly with the surrounding landscape, a testament to the harmonious coexistence between humans and nature.

Marveling at the natural beauty that unfolds around you, you'll feel a deep connection with the elements. The fresh breeze caresses your face, carrying with it the scents of the lake and the earth. The symphony of sounds—ripples of water, chirping birds, rustling leaves—creates a melodic backdrop that lulls you into a state of tranquility. The serenity of the lake becomes a sanctuary for contemplation and introspection, allowing you to escape the noise and chaos of the outside world.

As you continue your exploration, you may come across small fishing boats gliding across the water, their occupants expertly casting their nets in search of the lake's abundant fish. This traditional way of life, deeply intertwined with the rhythms of the lake, is a testament to the rich cultural heritage of the region. Observing the locals engage in their daily activities, you gain a newfound appreciation for the symbiotic relationship between the lake and its people—a relationship that has sustained generations and continues to shape the identity of the communities that thrive along its shores.

Whether you choose to bask in the sun's warm embrace on a leisurely boat ride or embark on a kayaking adventure to explore the hidden corners of the lake, each moment spent on Lake Atitlán is an opportunity to immerse yourself in its natural wonders. You become a witness to the interplay between land, water, and sky, where the elements converge in perfect harmony. It is a testament to the power and beauty of nature, reminding us of our place in the grand tapestry of the universe.

As the sun begins its descent, casting a golden glow across the lake's surface, you witness a breathtaking sunset that paints the sky in hues of orange, pink, and purple. The tranquil waters mirror the spectacle above, creating a surreal tableau that feels like a glimpse into another realm. The magic of Lake Atitlán is not limited to daylight hours—the lake takes on a different persona as twilight descends, revealing a serene and mysterious allure that captivates the soul.

As you bid farewell to Lake Atitlán, you carry with you a sense of wonder and gratitude for the experience you have had. The shimmering blue waters, the majestic volcanoes, and the picturesque landscapes will forever be etched in your memory. Lake Atitlán is not merely a destination; it is a sanctuary that invites you to reconnect with nature, to embrace the beauty that surrounds you, and to find solace in the simplicity of life.

Exploring Indigenous Villages and Traditions

Surrounding Lake Atitlán are several indigenous villages, each offering a captivating glimpse into their distinct culture, traditions, and handicrafts. These villages provide an enriching experience for travelers seeking to immerse themselves in the daily life of the locals, learn about their customs, and support the community by purchasing authentic handmade crafts. Let's explore two prominent villages: San Juan la Laguna and Santiago Atitlán.

San Juan la Laguna is a charming village known for its vibrant textile industry. As you arrive, you'll be greeted by the colorful streets lined with textile cooperatives and workshops. The village is home to skilled weavers who continue to practice traditional techniques passed down through generations. Take the opportunity to witness the intricate process of weaving and dyeing fabrics using natural materials such as plant extracts and cochineal insects. Many cooperative workshops offer demonstrations where you can observe the skilled artisans at work, weaving intricate patterns on backstrap looms.

Engaging with the locals in San Juan la Laguna provides a deeper understanding of the cultural significance of textiles in their lives. Strike up conversations with the weavers, who are often more than happy to share their stories and explain the symbolism behind the patterns and colors used in their textiles. This exchange not only enhances your appreciation for their craftsmanship but also creates a meaningful connection between cultures.

Beyond textiles, San Juan la Laguna is renowned for its commitment to sustainable practices. The village is known for its organic coffee production, where you can witness the entire process, from coffee bean cultivation to the roasting and brewing methods. Visit coffee plantations and learn about the principles of fair trade and ecological awareness that shape their production.

Another village of great cultural significance is Santiago Atitlán, which offers a glimpse into the spiritual practices of the Tz'utujil Maya. This village holds a deep connection to its ancient traditions and rituals, which are still very much alive today. One of the most revered sites in Santiago Atitlán is the Maximon shrine, a syncretic deity that blends elements of Catholicism with Mayan beliefs. Maximon is considered a powerful and protective figure, and the shrine dedicated to him is a focal point of spiritual life in the village.

Visiting the Maximon shrine offers a unique opportunity to witness the syncretic blend of religious practices. Observe the rituals performed by local shamans and devotees, who offer prayers, burn incense, and present offerings to seek guidance or express gratitude. The atmosphere is alive with devotion, and it's an incredible experience to witness the profound spiritual connection between the Tz'utujil Maya and their beliefs.

In addition to the Maximon shrine, Santiago Atitlán is known for its vibrant market, where locals gather to buy and sell a wide array of goods. The market is a bustling hub of activity, filled with vendors showcasing handmade crafts, fresh produce, and local delicacies. Take your time to wander through the stalls, appreciating the intricate beaded jewelry, vibrant textiles, and intricately carved wooden crafts. Engaging in conversations with the artisans and vendors allows you to gain insight into their techniques, inspirations, and the significance of their creations.

By supporting the local community through the purchase of authentic handmade crafts, you contribute to the preservation of traditional artistic practices and economic sustainability. The impact of your support extends beyond the immediate transaction, as it helps to ensure the continuation of these cultural traditions for future generations.

Immersing yourself in the daily life of the locals in San Juan la Laguna and Santiago Atitlán is a transformative experience. Through direct interactions and a genuine interest in their customs, you can forge connections that transcend cultural boundaries. By supporting their artistic endeavors and sustainable practices, you play an active role in preserving the cultural heritage of these indigenous communities.

As you explore these villages, allow yourself to be captivated by the beauty of their craftsmanship, the depth of their spirituality, and the warmth of their hospitality. The cultural immersion in San Juan la Laguna and Santiago Atitlán will leave an indelible mark on your journey, fostering a deep appreciation for the rich tapestry of indigenous cultures that thrive in the heart of Guatemala's Lake Atitlán region.

Outdoor Adventures and Water Activities

Lake Atitlán, a true haven for adventure enthusiasts, offers an extensive array of thrilling outdoor activities that are sure to ignite your sense of adventure. Whether you're seeking panoramic views from towering volcanoes, exploring the lush landscapes on guided treks, or immersing yourself in the crystal-clear waters of the lake, Lake Atitlán is a playground waiting to be explored.

One of the most exhilarating experiences at Lake Atitlán is hiking to the summit of San Pedro Volcano. Rising over 9,900 feet (3,020 meters) above sea level, this dormant volcano offers an unforgettable adventure. The trek to the top is challenging but immensely rewarding, as you ascend through ever-changing ecosystems. As you hike, the scenery transforms from coffee plantations to dense cloud forests, creating a sense of awe and wonder. Once you reach the summit, you'll be greeted by breathtaking panoramic views of the entire lake and the surrounding landscapes. The sight of the sparkling blue waters, the verdant hills, and the neighboring volcanoes is simply awe-inspiring, making the effort to reach the top well worth it.

If you prefer to explore the natural wonders surrounding Lake Atitlán at a more leisurely pace, embark on a guided trek through the lush coffee plantations and cloud forests. Immerse yourself in the beauty of the region as you traverse winding paths, passing by rows of coffee bushes heavy with ripening beans. Learn about the traditional cultivation and processing methods used to produce some of Guatemala's finest coffee. Breathe in the fresh mountain air and listen to the sounds of nature as your knowledgeable guide shares insights into the local flora and fauna. These treks provide a unique opportunity to witness the region's biodiversity up close and to appreciate the delicate balance of the ecosystem that sustains it.

For those drawn to the water, Lake Atitlán offers a paradise for swimming, snorkeling, and diving. Dive into the crystal-clear waters, where visibility can reach impressive depths, and discover the fascinating underwater world that lies beneath the surface. The lake is home to a diverse array of aquatic life, including colorful fish, freshwater sponges, and even ancient Mayan artifacts that rest on the lake's floor. Snorkel along the shores, exploring the vibrant reefs and marvelling at the kaleidoscope of marine life. Swim in the calm, refreshing waters, feeling the gentle currents embrace you. Whether you're an experienced diver or a novice snorkeler, Lake Atitlán's underwater wonders are sure to captivate and leave you with unforgettable memories.

One of the most magical experiences at Lake Atitlán is witnessing the captivating sunrise or sunset over the tranquil waters. As the first rays of the sun pierce through the morning mist, the lake gradually awakens, transforming into a symphony of colors. The sky is painted in hues of gold, pink, and purple, casting a magical glow over the surrounding volcanoes and hills. Find a serene spot along the lakeside, breathe in the fresh morning air, and watch as the world comes alive in the soft, warm light. Similarly, as the sun begins to set, the lake becomes a canvas for an awe-inspiring display of colors. The fiery oranges, deep purples, and gentle blues create a breathtaking spectacle that reflects upon the water's surface. Allow yourself to be swept away by the beauty of nature as you witness these ethereal moments at Lake Atitlán.

Beyond these thrilling activities, Lake Atitlán also presents opportunities for paragliding, kayaking, and paddleboarding. Soar through the skies on a paragliding adventure and experience the exhilaration of gliding above the lake, taking in panoramic views of the surrounding landscapes. Rent a kayak or paddleboard and explore the tranquil waters at your own pace, stopping to admire hidden coves, swim in secluded spots, and connect with the serenity of the lake. The gentle rhythm of your paddle, the lapping of the water against your craft, and the peaceful ambiance create a sense of tranquility that is truly unmatched.

Lake Atitlán is a destination that caters to adventure seekers of all levels. Whether you're an experienced mountaineer, an avid hiker, or simply someone who enjoys immersing themselves in nature, the possibilities for adventure are endless. From conquering the summit of San Pedro Volcano to embarking on guided treks through coffee plantations and cloud forests, Lake Atitlán offers a diverse range of landscapes to explore. For water enthusiasts, the crystal-clear waters of the lake beckon with opportunities for swimming, snorkeling, and diving. And let's not forget the magical experience of witnessing the sunrise or sunset, where nature paints the sky with a palette of colors that leave you in awe.

Lake Atitlán is a true adventurer's playground, where the beauty of nature intertwines with thrilling activities, creating an experience that will stay with you long after your journey ends. So, seize the opportunity to delve into the wonders that await at Lake Atitlán, and let your spirit of adventure guide you as you uncover the magic of this remarkable destination.

Spiritual and Wellness Experiences

Lake Atitlán has long been revered as a spiritual haven, drawing seekers from around the world who are in search of inner peace, self-discovery, and a deeper connection with nature. The serene surroundings of the lake, nestled among towering volcanoes and lush hills, provide an idyllic setting for those seeking solace and spiritual growth.

One of the most popular ways to embark on a spiritual journey at Lake Atitlán is by joining a yoga retreat or meditation session. Numerous lakeside retreat centers offer a variety of programs tailored to different levels and interests. Whether you are a beginner or an experienced practitioner, you can find retreats that cater to your needs. Imagine waking up to the gentle lapping of the lake's waters, breathing in the fresh mountain air, and starting your day with a rejuvenating yoga practice or a peaceful meditation session. Experienced instructors guide you through asanas (postures), pranayama (breathing techniques), and meditation, helping you cultivate mindfulness, balance, and self-awareness. The tranquil ambiance of Lake Atitlán enhances the transformative effects of these practices, allowing you to dive deeper into your spiritual journey.

In addition to yoga and meditation, Lake Atitlán offers a rich tapestry of holistic healing practices that can nourish your mind, body, and spirit. Retreat centers and wellness spas provide an array of treatments and therapies that draw inspiration from ancient traditions and local wisdom. Reiki, a Japanese energy healing technique, helps restore balance and harmony by channeling universal life force energy. Under the guidance of skilled practitioners, you can experience the subtle yet powerful effects of Reiki, promoting relaxation, stress reduction, and energetic healing.

Sound baths have also gained popularity as a means of healing and deep relaxation at Lake Atitlán. Sound healing practitioners utilize various instruments such as Tibetan singing bowls, crystal bowls, gongs, and chimes to create soothing and harmonious vibrations. As you lie or sit in a comfortable position, the gentle sounds and vibrations wash over you, creating a sense of tranquility and allowing your mind and body to enter a meditative state. Sound baths can help release energetic blockages, promote emotional well-being, and enhance your connection with the present moment.

For those seeking a more immersive experience, traditional Mayan ceremonies offer a profound connection with the indigenous cultures and ancient wisdom of the region. The Mayans have a deep reverence for nature and its elements, and their ceremonies often incorporate rituals, prayers, and offerings to honor the natural world. Cacao ceremonies, for example, involve drinking ceremonial-grade cacao prepared with intention and mindfulness. Cacao, considered a sacred plant medicine, is believed to open the heart and facilitate a deeper spiritual connection. Participants come together in a sacred circle, guided by a Mayan shaman or ceremonial leader, to experience the transformative and heart-opening effects of cacao.

Temazcal ceremonies, also known as sweat lodge ceremonies, are another ancient Mayan tradition that has been preserved and passed down through generations. Participants enter a dome-shaped structure made of natural materials, symbolizing the womb of Mother Earth. Heated stones are placed in the center, and water infused with medicinal herbs is poured over them, creating steam and a purifying heat. The ceremony is a deeply cleansing and purifying experience, both physically and energetically, as participants release toxins, negative emotions, and stagnant energy. The heat and darkness of the temazcal represent a symbolic journey of rebirth and transformation, allowing participants to emerge with a renewed sense of clarity, strength, and spiritual connection.

Lake Atitlán and its surroundings provide an immersive and transformative environment for spiritual seekers. The sacred energy of the lake, the majestic volcanoes, and the vibrant indigenous culture all contribute to a deeply enriching experience. Whether you choose to embark on a yoga retreat, indulge in holistic healing practices, or participate in traditional Mayan ceremonies, Lake Atitlán offers a sanctuary where you can find solace, gain insights, and reconnect with your inner self. The combination of the natural beauty, cultural heritage, and spiritual traditions of this magical place creates a unique opportunity for personal growth, self-reflection, and spiritual awakening.

Chapter 6: Tikal and the Ancient Maya Civilization

Introduction to Tikal National Park

Tikal National Park is a testament to the remarkable ancient Maya civilization and stands as a beacon of its rich historical and cultural legacy. Situated in the northern region of Guatemala, Tikal is not only a UNESCO World Heritage Site but also one of the most significant archaeological sites in the Maya world. With a history that spans over 2,000 years, this extraordinary place immerses visitors in a journey back in time, surrounded by the remnants of a once-thriving city adorned with towering pyramids, grand temples, and enveloped by a lush rainforest.

Encompassing a vast expanse of approximately 575 square kilometers (222 square miles), Tikal National Park holds within its borders the remnants of the ancient city of Tikal. This sprawling archaeological complex was once a thriving hub of Maya civilization. During the Classic Period from 200 to 900 AD, Tikal reached its zenith, serving as a vital center for politics, economy, and religion. At its peak, the city boasted a population of over 90,000 inhabitants, a testament to its prominence and influence.

As you step foot into Tikal, you'll find yourself immersed in the grandeur of the ancient city. The towering pyramids, such as Temple I (also known as the Temple of the Great Jaguar) and Temple II (known as the Temple of the Masks), are awe-inspiring architectural marvels that showcase the ingenuity and artistic prowess of the Maya civilization. These structures served as sacred sites for religious ceremonies and provided a connection between the mortal world and the divine realms.

Wandering through the plazas, ball courts, and royal palaces, visitors can gain a glimpse into the daily life and cultural practices of the ancient Maya. The layout of the city reveals meticulous planning and organization, with residential areas, administrative buildings, and ceremonial spaces each playing a vital role in the functioning of the city. The well-preserved stelae and altars provide insights into the history, genealogy, and achievements of the Maya rulers who once reigned here.

Beyond its archaeological significance, Tikal National Park is also a sanctuary for biodiversity. The park is nestled within the Maya Biosphere Reserve, a protected area that encompasses vast stretches of lush rainforest and is home to a remarkable array of plant and animal species. As visitors explore the park's trails, they are greeted by the symphony of nature, with the calls of howler monkeys echoing through the trees and vibrant bird species fluttering overhead. The park is also home to elusive and majestic creatures like the jaguar and ocelot, reminding us of the diverse and fragile ecosystem that thrives within its boundaries.

Tikal's magnificence extends beyond its immediate borders. The park serves as a gateway to nearby archaeological sites and natural parks that further enrich the exploration of the region. Just a short distance away lies Yaxha, another captivating Maya city adorned with temples and offering panoramic views of the picturesque Yaxha Lagoon. Exploring Yaxha allows visitors to witness the interconnectedness of ancient Maya settlements and their shared cultural heritage.

For nature enthusiasts, a visit to Biotopo Cerro Cahui is highly recommended. This protected area provides an opportunity to immerse oneself in the pristine beauty of the Guatemalan rainforest. With hiking trails that wind through dense vegetation and meander along the shores of the tranquil Petexbatun Lagoon, visitors can encounter a variety of wildlife, including colorful birds, reptiles, and mammals.

Venturing deeper into the wilderness, the intrepid traveler may choose to embark on a multi-day trek to the remote archaeological site of El Mirador. Known as the "Lost City of the Maya," El Mirador is still in the process of being excavated, revealing the grandeur and complexity of an ancient city that once rivaled Tikal. The journey to El Mirador is an adventure in itself, navigating through dense jungle and traversing ancient causeways, but the reward is an encounter with the vestiges of a civilization that remains partially shrouded in mystery.

Tikal National Park is not merely a historical site or a natural reserve—it is a living testament to the ingenuity, creativity, and cultural richness of the Maya civilization. It allows visitors to step into the footsteps of the past, to connect with the spirits of those who once inhabited this magnificent city. Tikal's towering pyramids, grand temples, and lush rainforest serve as reminders of the resilience and enduring legacy of the Maya people, inviting us to appreciate and preserve this extraordinary heritage for generations to come.

Exploring the Majestic Tikal Ruins

Prepare to be transported back in time as you step into the ancient ruins of Tikal. This UNESCO World Heritage Site is a testament to the ingenuity and artistic prowess of the ancient

Maya civilization. As you explore the sprawling complex, you'll be awe-inspired by the towering pyramids and intricate architectural structures that dominate the landscape, showcasing the advanced engineering skills of the Maya.

One of the most iconic and impressive structures in Tikal is Temple I, also known as the Temple of the Great Jaguar. This majestic pyramid stands as a symbol of power and reverence, its grandeur evident in every meticulously carved stone. As you ascend its steep steps, you can't help but feel a sense of anticipation. Finally, reaching the top, you are greeted with a breathtaking panoramic view of the surrounding jungle canopy. The sight is awe-inspiring, and you can't help but appreciate the architectural brilliance that allowed the Maya to construct such monumental structures in the heart of the dense rainforest.

Another notable structure that demands attention is Temple II, commonly referred to as the Temple of the Masks. This temple features a series of intricate stucco masks depicting the deities and rulers of the Maya civilization. Each mask tells a story, a glimpse into the ancient beliefs and mythology that shaped the lives of the Maya people. Standing before these beautifully adorned masks, you can't help but marvel at the artistic finesse and attention to detail that went into their creation. They serve as a testament to the spiritual significance that permeated every aspect of Maya life.

Temple III offers a different perspective, allowing visitors to witness the remnants of elaborate religious rituals that were once performed by the Maya. This temple, although partially restored, still exudes an air of mystique and offers valuable insights into the ceremonial practices of this ancient civilization. As you wander through the plazas, ball courts, and royal palaces, you begin to piece together the fragments of daily life in Tikal. The ancient structures come alive with whispers of past conversations, laughter, and celebrations. You can almost envision the bustling activity that once animated these grand structures.

The plazas, with their open spaces and surrounding structures, were the heart of Tikal's social and civic life. It was here that the Maya people gathered for ceremonial events, trade, and community gatherings. As you walk through these historic plazas, you can imagine the vibrant colors that once adorned the temples and the echoes of ritual chants that filled the air during sacred ceremonies. The ball courts, where the Maya played their traditional ballgame, offer a glimpse into the sporting events and cultural practices that brought the community together.

The royal palaces, with their intricate architectural features and ornate decorations, provide a window into the lives of Tikal's elite. These structures were not only residences for the ruling class but also served as administrative and ceremonial centers. Exploring the inner chambers and courtyards of these palaces, you can envision the opulence and grandeur that once characterized Maya royalty. The detailed carvings and intricate murals tell stories of power, lineage, and spiritual connections.

As you immerse yourself in the ruins of Tikal, you'll gain a deeper understanding of the Maya people's daily life, spiritual beliefs, and societal structure. The ancient city whispers its secrets to those who listen, offering a glimpse into a civilization that flourished in the heart of the Central American jungle. Tikal's ruins stand as a testament to the resilience and ingenuity of the Maya, their legacy preserved for generations to come.

Visiting Tikal is not just a journey through ancient history; it is a spiritual and transformative experience. The weight of centuries of human existence hangs in the air, and as you wander among the ruins, you can't help but feel a deep connection to the past. The beauty and intricacy of the architecture, the stories etched into every stone, and the natural splendor of the surrounding jungle all combine to create a truly unforgettable experience.

So prepare yourself to be awe-inspired as you embark on this journey into the majestic ruins of Tikal. Let the towering pyramids and remarkable structures ignite your imagination and transport you to a time long gone. Discover the stories, unravel the mysteries, and gain a newfound appreciation for the ancient Maya civilization. Tikal beckons, ready to share its treasures and secrets with those who seek to explore its extraordinary past.

Wildlife and Nature in Tikal

Prepare to be awe-inspired as you step into the world of Tikal, a place where the ancient Maya civilization comes alive through majestic ruins and incredible architectural structures. Located within the sprawling Tikal National Park, this archaeological site showcases the advanced engineering and artistic skills of the Maya people, leaving visitors captivated by the grandeur of their achievements.

As you approach the site, you'll be greeted by towering pyramids that pierce the sky, a testament to the ambitious vision and technical expertise of the Maya architects. Among the remarkable structures in Tikal is Temple I, known as the Temple of the Great Jaguar. This iconic pyramid rises above the surrounding landscape, its steep steps beckoning you to embark on a climb that promises not only physical exertion but also an unparalleled reward.

Ascending the steps of Temple I, you'll feel a sense of anticipation building within you. As you reach the summit, a breathtaking panorama unfolds before your eyes. The sprawling expanse of the dense jungle stretches out in every direction, its lush green canopy extending as far as the eye can see. The sight is nothing short of mesmerizing, and it's easy to imagine how the Maya priests and rulers must have felt, standing atop this sacred structure, surveying their realm.

Adjacent to Temple I is Temple II, also known as the Temple of the Masks. This distinctive pyramid is adorned with intricate carvings and stucco decorations, depicting the enigmatic faces of ancient Maya gods and rulers. Each mask tells a story, a glimpse into the religious beliefs and mythological narratives that shaped the lives of the Maya people. As you wander through the ancient plazas and courtyards, you'll encounter remnants of a civilization that once thrived in this very place.

Temple III, another notable structure, offers insight into the elaborate religious rituals performed by the Maya. As you explore its weathered staircases and explore its hidden chambers, you'll gain a deeper understanding of the spiritual beliefs and practices that were central to Maya society. The remnants of altars and sacrificial platforms speak volumes about the reverence and devotion the Maya held for their gods.

Beyond the architectural marvels, Tikal National Park is a haven of natural beauty and biodiversity. The park forms part of the larger Maya Biosphere Reserve, a vast protected area that safeguards numerous plant and animal species. The dense rainforest that envelops the ruins is a vibrant ecosystem teeming with life, offering a unique opportunity for nature enthusiasts and wildlife lovers.

As you traverse the trails that wind through the park, an orchestra of sounds fills the air. The deep guttural calls of howler monkeys reverberate through the treetops, signaling their presence in the canopy above. Colorful toucans perch on branches, their vibrant feathers adding splashes of brilliance to the green surroundings. Meanwhile, coatis, agile and curious creatures, scurry along the forest floor, their bandit-like masks adding a touch of whimsy to the scene.

Tikal is not only a sanctuary for these creatures but also provides refuge for elusive predators such as jaguars and ocelots. Though rarely seen, their presence is a testament to the park's intact ecosystem and the conservation efforts in place. Birdwatchers will also find themselves in paradise, as Tikal is home to a diverse array of bird species. With patience and a keen eye, you may spot resplendent quetzals, elegant herons, or the vibrant plumage of tropical birds darting through the foliage.

The symbiotic relationship between the archaeological wonders and the natural splendor of Tikal creates a truly immersive experience. As you wander through the ancient plazas, ball courts, and royal palaces, you'll find yourself transported back in time, gaining intimate glimpses into the daily life, cultural practices, and spiritual beliefs of the Maya people.

Every step in Tikal is a reminder of the profound connection between humanity and nature, a testament to the enduring legacy of the ancient Maya civilization. It is a place where history and the natural world intertwine, leaving an indelible mark on all who have the privilege of exploring its wonders.

Nearby Archaeological Sites and Natural Parks

In addition to the wonders of Tikal, the surrounding area offers a wealth of archaeological sites and natural parks to explore. Just a short distance from Tikal is the site of Yaxha, another ancient Maya city that will transport you back in time and immerse you in the captivating history of the region. Yaxha, meaning "green water," is aptly named as it overlooks the picturesque Yaxha Lagoon, adding to the site's charm and beauty.

As you venture through Yaxha, you'll encounter impressive temples, plazas, and ceremonial complexes that reflect the architectural brilliance of the Maya civilization. The site features two main acropolises, known as North Acropolis and East Acropolis, which were once centers of political and religious activities. Climb to the top of the pyramids for breathtaking panoramic views of the surrounding jungle and the shimmering lagoon. Witnessing a sunset from one of these elevated vantage points is a truly magical experience.

The allure of Yaxha extends beyond its archaeological ruins. The site is nestled within the Yaxha-Nakum-Naranjo National Park, a protected area known for its abundant flora and fauna. As you explore the park, you'll traverse lush forests and encounter a diverse array of wildlife, including howler monkeys, toucans, and colorful butterflies. The park also offers hiking trails that meander along the shores of the beautiful Petexbatun Lagoon, providing ample opportunities to connect with nature and soak in the tranquil surroundings.

For nature lovers, a visit to the nearby Biotopo Cerro Cahui is an absolute must. This biological reserve is dedicated to the preservation of the region's unique ecosystems and serves as a haven for countless plant and animal species. The reserve is characterized by its dense forests, vibrant birdlife, and the mesmerizing Petexbatun Lagoon. Hiking trails crisscross the reserve, offering visitors the chance to immerse themselves in the natural wonders of Guatemala. Birdwatchers will be delighted by the opportunity to spot rare and colorful avian species, while nature enthusiasts can revel in the beauty of the flora and fauna that thrive within this protected sanctuary.

Another notable nearby destination is the lesser-known site of El Mirador, located deep within the heart of the Guatemalan jungle. El Mirador is a remote archaeological site that is still undergoing excavation, but it is already revealing the secrets of an ancient Maya city that once rivaled Tikal in size and grandeur. Visiting El Mirador is a true adventure, as it requires a multi-day trek through dense, untouched wilderness. However, the rewards for those who embark on this journey are truly priceless.

As you traverse the challenging terrain and navigate through the thick jungle, you'll be rewarded with the sight of monumental pyramids, towering structures, and intricate stucco carvings that offer insights into the life and culture of the ancient Maya. The most prominent structure at El Mirador is La Danta, one of the largest pyramids in the world, which stands as a testament to the architectural genius of the ancient Maya civilization. From the summit of La Danta, you can gaze upon the vast expanse of the jungle, feeling a profound sense of connection to the past and an appreciation for the remarkable achievements of the Maya.

El Mirador is more than an archaeological site; it is an immersive experience that allows you to step back in time and truly understand the grandeur and complexity of the ancient Maya civilization. The journey to El Mirador is physically demanding but spiritually rewarding, providing a profound sense of adventure and discovery.

Whether you choose to focus your exploration on Tikal, uncover the mysteries of Yaxha, immerse yourself in the natural wonders of Biotopo Cerro Cahui, or embark on the epic adventure to El Mirador, the ancient Maya civilization and the wonders of the Guatemalan jungle await you with open arms. Each site offers a unique perspective on the rich history, vibrant culture, and awe-inspiring beauty of Guatemala. Prepare to be captivated by the remnants of a glorious past and enchanted by the raw power of nature as you delve into the heart of this extraordinary region.

Chapter 7: The Pacific Coast and Beach Destinations

Beaches and Surfing Spots

The Pacific Coast of Guatemala beckons travelers with its exquisite array of beaches and world-class surfing spots. As you venture along the coast, you'll discover pristine stretches of sand, turquoise waters, and the perfect waves for riding. Whether you're a seasoned surfer seeking thrilling breaks or a beginner looking to catch your first wave, the Pacific Coast of Guatemala offers an incredible surfing experience for surfers of all levels.

One of the most popular beach destinations along the Pacific Coast is Monterrico. This vibrant beach town attracts locals and tourists alike with its lively atmosphere and beautiful coastline. The black volcanic sand of Monterrico's beaches provides a unique backdrop, creating a stunning contrast against the clear blue waters. The waves here are known for their consistency, making it an excellent spot for both beginners and experienced surfers. If you're new to surfing, there are surf schools and experienced instructors available to guide you through the basics and help you catch your first wave. For seasoned surfers, Monterrico offers exciting breaks that will satisfy your craving for adrenaline.

For those seeking a more secluded and tranquil beach experience, Champerico is a hidden gem. This off-the-beaten-path paradise boasts pristine beaches fringed by coconut palms and mangroves. The laid-back ambiance and untouched beauty of Champerico make it an ideal destination for relaxation and surf exploration. The waves here cater to both intermediate and advanced surfers, providing the perfect setting for challenging rides or honing your skills.

As you explore the Pacific Coast, you'll encounter a multitude of other enchanting beaches, each with its own distinct character. El Paredón, situated between the ocean and a mangrove lagoon, is a picturesque beach that captivates visitors with its natural beauty and peaceful surroundings. It is renowned for its consistent waves, making it a favorite spot for surfers seeking thrilling rides. Further south, Sipacate offers a pristine beachfront that stretches for miles, where you can enjoy long walks and take in breathtaking sunsets. The waves here are suitable for surfers of various levels, providing an opportunity for both learning and progression.

Apart from surfing, the beaches along the Pacific Coast of Guatemala offer a wide range of activities for everyone to enjoy. Sunbathing enthusiasts can lay their beach towels on the soft sands, soaking up the tropical sun while listening to the gentle crashing of waves. Beach volleyball courts are scattered along the shoreline, inviting visitors to engage in friendly matches or simply watch the spirited games. Families with children can revel in the joy of building sandcastles and playing in the shallow waters. The beaches also provide ample space for picnics, where you can savor local delicacies while taking in the breathtaking coastal views.

When you're not in the water, take a leisurely stroll along the beach, immersing yourself in the coastal ambiance and observing the local life. Beach vendors offer an array of snacks and refreshing drinks, allowing you to indulge in the flavors of the region while supporting the local economy. If you're lucky, you may even witness local fishermen casting their nets or bringing in their daily catch, providing an authentic glimpse into the traditional fishing culture of the area.

In addition to the popular surf spots and beach activities, the Pacific Coast of Guatemala offers a diverse range of experiences for travelers to enjoy. Beyond the sandy shores, you can venture into the surrounding areas and discover a world of natural wonders, cultural attractions, and delicious culinary experiences.

Nature enthusiasts will find solace in the coastal ecosystems and wildlife reserves that dot the region. Take a boat tour through the mangrove forests of the Biotopo Monterrico-Hawaii Nature Reserve, a protected area teeming with biodiversity. Here, you can observe a wide variety of bird species, including herons, egrets, and pelicans, as well as reptiles such as turtles and crocodiles. The reserve also serves as a nesting ground for several species of sea turtles, and if you're fortunate, you may witness the awe-inspiring sight of baby turtles making their way to the ocean.

For a more immersive nature experience, head to the Hawaii National Park, located near the town of Tulate. This national park encompasses both volcanic landscapes and marine environments, offering a unique combination of natural beauty. Embark on a hike through lush trails that wind through the tropical forest, and keep an eye out for exotic bird species and other wildlife along the way. As you reach the coastline, you'll be rewarded with breathtaking views of the ocean and opportunities for snorkeling to explore the vibrant underwater world.

Coastal towns and fishing villages along the Pacific Coast provide an authentic glimpse into the local culture and way of life. Puerto San José, a bustling port town, is renowned for its vibrant fish market, where you can witness the fishermen's daily activities and sample the freshest seafood. Explore the waterfront area, where you'll find an array of seafood restaurants serving up delicious ceviche, grilled fish, and other coastal delicacies.

Further south, the charming fishing village of Iztapa offers a tranquil and serene atmosphere. Walk along the shoreline and admire the colorful fishing boats swaying gently in the water. Engage with the friendly locals, who are always eager to share stories about their fishing traditions and daily life in the village. If you're lucky, you may even have the opportunity to join a fishing excursion and experience the thrill of catching your own dinner.

When it comes to cuisine, the Pacific Coast of Guatemala boasts a rich culinary heritage influenced by both the ocean and the surrounding land. Seafood lovers will delight in the abundance of fresh catches, from shrimp and snapper to lobster and octopus. Don't miss the opportunity to indulge in a traditional seafood platter, complete with grilled fish, ceviche, and coconut-infused rice.

For those seeking a taste of the region's land-based cuisine, you can savor traditional dishes such as "subanik," a hearty stew made with indigenous ingredients like chayote squash and chipilín leaves. Corn-based dishes, such as "tamales" and "tortillas," are staples of Guatemalan cuisine and are often enjoyed with a side of "hilachas" or "pepian," two flavorful meat stews.

As the day draws to a close, take a moment to witness the mesmerizing sunsets that grace the Pacific Coast. Find a tranquil spot along the beach, perhaps with a refreshing drink in hand, and watch as the vibrant hues of orange and pink paint the sky, casting a warm glow over the ocean. These magical moments are a testament to the natural beauty and serenity that can be found along the shores of Guatemala's Pacific Coast.

Whether you're seeking thrilling surf adventures, tranquil beachside relaxation, immersion in local culture, or a combination of all three, the Pacific Coast of Guatemala offers a captivating experience for every traveler. With its stunning beaches, diverse wildlife, authentic coastal communities, and delectable cuisine, this region is sure to leave a lasting impression and create cherished memories of your journey through Guatemala.

Ecotourism and Wildlife Reserves

Beyond the beaches, the Pacific Coast of Guatemala beckons with its mesmerizing ecotourism destinations and wildlife reserves. These protected areas serve as havens for a remarkable array of flora and fauna, providing visitors with the opportunity to immerse themselves in the natural beauty of the region.

One such captivating destination is the Biotopo Monterrico-Hawaii Nature Reserve, boasting extensive mangrove forests that harbor an extraordinary ecosystem. As you step into this enchanting realm, you'll find yourself surrounded by lush greenery and the melodies of countless bird species. The reserve is a sanctuary for migratory birds, making it a paradise for birdwatching enthusiasts. With patience and a keen eye, you may spot colorful herons, majestic frigatebirds, and elusive roseate spoonbills among the branches.

The Biotopo Monterrico-Hawaii Nature Reserve also plays a crucial role in the conservation of sea turtles. These magnificent creatures find solace in the reserve's protected beaches, where they nest and lay their eggs. Witnessing the nesting habits of sea turtles is a truly awe-inspiring experience, as you observe these ancient marine reptiles fulfilling their instinctual rituals. Guided boat tours through the mangroves offer a unique perspective on the importance of these ecosystems in supporting the coastal environment. Knowledgeable guides will enlighten you about the delicate balance between the mangroves and the surrounding ecosystems, highlighting their role in protecting the coastline from erosion and providing vital habitats for numerous species.

Traveling further south along the Pacific Coast, you'll encounter the remarkable Hawaii National Park. Named after the indigenous hawia trees that thrive in the area, this park is a testament to the region's rich biodiversity. Hawaii National Park encompasses both volcanic landscapes and marine environments, offering an incredible range of outdoor activities and natural wonders.

Embarking on a hike within the park unveils the striking contrast between ancient lava fields and lush vegetation. As you traverse the trails, the vibrant colors of endemic flowers and plants will captivate your senses. Look out for bromeliads, orchids, and ferns, which thrive in the park's fertile volcanic soil. The park's volcanic past is also evident in its geological features, including extinct craters, lava tubes, and lava flows frozen in time. Exploring these volcanic formations provides a fascinating glimpse into the dynamic forces that have shaped the region over millennia.

Nature lovers and bird enthusiasts will be delighted by the diverse avian population that calls the Hawaii National Park home. Binoculars in hand, you may spot resplendent quetzals, scarlet macaws, and the vibrant blue-crowned motmot. The park is also home to an array of hummingbird species, which flit gracefully from flower to flower, their iridescent feathers shimmering in the sunlight.

For those seeking an aquatic adventure, the marine environments surrounding Hawaii National Park offer an abundance of wonders beneath the waves. Snorkeling or diving in these crystal-clear waters presents an opportunity to encounter an array of marine life. Be mesmerized by the kaleidoscope of colors as tropical fish dart in and out of coral reefs. Keep an eye out for graceful sea turtles gracefully gliding through the water, and if luck is on your side, you may even witness pods of playful dolphins as they leap and dance in the ocean.

In addition to its natural splendors, Hawaii National Park is an ideal spot for enjoying picnics and leisurely walks along the pristine beaches. The rhythmic crashing of the waves provides a soothing soundtrack as you relax on the soft sand, basking in the warm coastal sun. The park's tranquil atmosphere invites you to unwind and connect with the beauty of your surroundings.

The Pacific Coast of Guatemala, with its mesmerizing ecotourism destinations and wildlife reserves, offers a gateway to nature's wonders. The Biotopo Monterrico-Hawaii Nature Reserve and the Hawaii National Park provide unique opportunities to delve into the diverse ecosystems of the region. Immerse yourself in the tranquility of the mangrove forests, observing the remarkable birdlife and the nesting habits of sea turtles. Explore the volcanic landscapes and underwater marvels of Hawaii National Park, discovering a world teeming with vibrant flora and fauna. Whether you're an avid nature enthusiast or simply seeking respite in the beauty of the natural world, the Pacific Coast of Guatemala will leave an indelible impression on your heart and soul.

Coastal Towns and Fishing Villages

Along the Pacific Coast of Guatemala, a captivating array of charming coastal towns and fishing villages awaits, offering visitors a unique glimpse into the local way of life. These communities, deeply connected to the ocean, rely on fishing as a primary source of livelihood, shaping their culture, traditions, and daily routines.

One such place to explore is Puerto San José, a bustling port town renowned for its vibrant fish market and lively waterfront. As you stroll through the market, your senses will be awakened by the sights, sounds, and aromas of the fresh catch of the day. Local fishermen bring in their hauls, showcasing an impressive variety of seafood, including fish, shrimp, lobster, and crab. Immerse yourself in the lively atmosphere as the market comes alive with the bustling activity of buyers and sellers negotiating prices and exchanging stories.

After perusing the market, make your way to one of the waterfront restaurants, where you can indulge in a true seafood feast. Sample delectable ceviche, a popular dish made with raw fish or seafood marinated in citrus juices and spices, resulting in a refreshing and flavorful culinary delight. Other seafood specialties, such as grilled fish or shrimp, prepared with local spices and accompanied by traditional sides like plantains and rice, provide a mouthwatering experience that highlights the region's culinary prowess.

As you dine, take in the captivating view of the waterfront, where colorful fishing boats dot the horizon. These boats, with their distinctive designs and vibrant hues, serve as a testament to the town's deep-rooted fishing traditions. Watch as fishermen meticulously prepare their vessels, ensuring they are ready to venture out into the vast ocean for their daily catch. Their expertise and knowledge of the sea have been passed down through generations, sustaining the livelihoods of the local community.

For those seeking a more tranquil coastal experience, the picturesque town of Iztapa beckons with its serene atmosphere and pristine beaches. Nestled along the Pacific coastline, Iztapa offers a peaceful retreat, far removed from the hustle and bustle of larger cities. As you arrive, you'll be greeted by the gentle rhythm of the waves and the soft, powdery sand beneath your feet.

Take a leisurely stroll along the shoreline, savoring the tranquility that envelops the area. Feel the warm embrace of the sun on your skin as you bask in the coastal serenity. The beaches of Iztapa are known for their natural beauty and unspoiled landscapes, making them ideal for relaxation and contemplation. Find a quiet spot to sit and admire the breathtaking scenery, as the azure waters of the Pacific Ocean meet the golden sands in a harmonious union.

As you explore the town, you'll notice the colorful fishing boats gracefully bobbing in the water. These vessels, adorned with vibrant paint and adorned with intricate details, reflect the artisanal craftsmanship and pride of the local fishermen. Engage with the friendly locals, who are eager to share stories of their seafaring adventures and the rich history of their community.

To truly immerse yourself in the tranquility of Iztapa, consider embarking on a boating excursion along the coastal waters. Sail alongside the fishermen as they cast their nets, skillfully navigating the currents to secure their bounty. Observe their time-honored fishing techniques and witness the harmony between man and nature as they work together to sustain their way of life.

Beyond the allure of the beaches and the fishing activities, Iztapa is also an excellent base for exploring the surrounding natural wonders. The nearby mangrove forests, with their intricate network of roots and abundant wildlife, provide an enchanting setting for eco-adventures. Take a boat tour through these mangroves, where you can witness the delicate balance of this unique ecosystem and spot a variety of bird species, including herons, kingfishers, and pelicans.

Additionally, Iztapa is known for its rich biodiversity, with various wildlife reserves in the vicinity. Birdwatchers will be delighted by the opportunity to observe rare and exotic species in their natural habitats. Keep your binoculars ready as you explore the wetlands and forests, where toucans, parrots, and hummingbirds display their vibrant plumage and enchanting songs.

In the evenings, as the sun begins its descent, find solace in the peaceful ambiance of Iztapa. Enjoy a leisurely stroll along the shoreline, allowing the gentle waves to serenade you. Witness the mesmerizing spectacle of the sky turning into a vibrant canvas, as hues of orange, pink, and purple paint a breathtaking panorama. This tranquil coastal town is the perfect setting to disconnect from the outside world, allowing you to reconnect with nature and find inner peace.

Puerto San José and Iztapa embody the essence of the Pacific Coast of Guatemala, each offering a distinct experience that showcases the deep-rooted connection between the local communities and the sea. Whether you choose to immerse yourself in the vibrant atmosphere of a bustling fish market or seek solace in the tranquility of a picturesque fishing village, these coastal destinations invite you to embrace the rich maritime heritage of Guatemala while experiencing the beauty and serenity of the Pacific Coast.

Relaxation and Beachside Activities

The Pacific Coast of Guatemala beckons travelers not only with its thrilling adventures and exploration opportunities but also with its serene and rejuvenating ambiance. After a day filled with exhilarating activities such as surfing, hiking, or exploring the region's natural wonders, it's essential to take some time to unwind and immerse oneself in the sheer beauty of the coast.

One of the most delightful ways to indulge in relaxation on the Pacific Coast is by treating yourself to a beachside massage. Imagine lying on a comfortable lounger, feeling the gentle breeze caress your skin, and hearing the rhythmic sound of the ocean waves in the background as skilled hands work their magic, kneading away any tension or stress accumulated during your adventures. These soothing massages can be found at various resorts and spas along the coast, providing a perfect opportunity to rejuvenate both your body and mind.

For those seeking a more holistic approach to relaxation, practicing yoga on the soft sand as the sun begins its descent can be an incredibly uplifting experience. The Pacific Coast's scenic vistas provide an ideal backdrop for reconnecting with your inner self and finding balance amidst the natural beauty that surrounds you. Join a beachfront yoga class led by experienced instructors who will guide you through a series of poses, allowing you to release any lingering stress and find serenity in the present moment. The combination of stretching, breathing exercises, and the calming sounds of the ocean will leave you feeling revitalized and grounded.

As the day winds down, there's no better way to fully embrace the coastal atmosphere than by indulging in a refreshing cocktail at a beachfront bar. Picture yourself sitting at a cozy table with your favorite tropical drink in hand, relishing the vibrant flavors and colors that encapsulate the essence of Guatemala. Let the ocean breeze gently brush against your skin as you listen to the symphony of crashing waves. This idyllic setting offers the perfect opportunity to unwind, share stories of your day's adventures with fellow travelers, or simply enjoy the peaceful solitude of the beach at sunset.

If you're in the mood for more active beachside activities, the Pacific Coast won't disappoint. Stand-up paddleboarding has gained popularity in recent years and provides an exciting way to explore the coastline while engaging your core muscles and improving balance. Glide across the calm waters, feeling a sense of freedom and connection with the vast expanse of the ocean. Alternatively, kayaking along the coast allows you to venture into hidden coves, discover secluded beaches, and witness marine life in their natural habitat. Paddle at your own pace, embracing the tranquility and immersing yourself in the breathtaking coastal landscapes that unfold before your eyes.

For those seeking pure relaxation without any particular activity in mind, there's no better way to unwind than by simply lying on a beach towel, book in hand, and letting the gentle rhythm of the ocean waves lull you into a state of pure bliss. Feel the warmth of the sun on your skin, breathe in the salty air, and lose yourself in the pages of a captivating novel. The Pacific Coast offers miles of pristine beaches where you can find your own slice of paradise, away from the hustle and bustle of everyday life. Embrace the slow pace, let time lose its significance, and allow the ebb and flow of the tides to guide your moments of pure relaxation.

Chapter 8: Guatemala's Cultural and Indigenous Heritage

Mayan Traditions and Indigenous Communities

One of the most remarkable aspects of Guatemala is its vibrant indigenous culture, deeply rooted in the ancient Mayan civilization that flourished in the region thousands of years ago. Today, the traditions, customs, and way of life of the Maya people continue to thrive, offering a captivating glimpse into their rich heritage. In this chapter, we invite you to delve into the tapestry of Mayan traditions and explore the diverse indigenous communities that call Guatemala home.

The Maya civilization, known for its advancements in architecture, mathematics, and astronomy, left an indelible mark on the region. While the ancient Maya cities have now turned into ruins scattered across the Guatemalan landscape, their legacy lives on through the customs and practices of their descendants. By immersing yourself in the daily lives of the Maya people, you can witness their deep connection to nature, their reverence for their ancestors, and their spiritual beliefs that intertwine with everyday existence.

One of the most striking aspects of Mayan culture is the significance of traditional clothing. Each indigenous community boasts its distinct attire, featuring intricate patterns and vibrant colors that not only showcase their identity but also represent their history and beliefs. For example, the women of the Maya community of

Chichicastenango wear elaborately woven huipiles, traditional blouses adorned with symbolic designs that tell stories of their ancestral lineage and cosmological beliefs. Every stitch and color choice is a deliberate expression of cultural heritage and serves as a visual tapestry connecting past and present.

Mayan rituals and practices, deeply ingrained in the fabric of everyday life, offer a fascinating insight into their spiritual beliefs. For instance, the ceremony of the Mayan fire ritual, known as the "Ch'ulel," is performed to establish harmony and balance between the natural and supernatural realms. This ancient tradition involves creating altars adorned with offerings of fruits, flowers, and candles, as well as the burning of copal, a resinous incense with sacred significance. The smoke is believed to carry prayers and messages to the deities, facilitating communication between the physical and spiritual worlds.

Similarly, the Maya sacred calendar, known as the "Cholq'ij," governs the lives of many indigenous communities. Composed of 260 days, each with its unique energy and meaning, the Cholq'ij guides important decisions, such as agricultural activities, personal events, and community celebrations. By understanding this calendar, one can appreciate the intricate relationship between the Maya people and the cyclical patterns of nature.

Furthermore, the Maya people's strong connection to nature is evident in their agricultural practices and reverence for the environment. Many communities maintain a sustainable way of farming, utilizing ancient techniques such as terracing and crop rotation. By working in harmony with the land, the Maya people showcase their respect for the Earth and its resources, recognizing the interdependence between human beings and the natural world.

To gain a deeper understanding of the Maya culture, it is essential to engage with the diverse indigenous communities across Guatemala. Visiting towns such as Santiago Atitlán, Todos Santos Cuchumatán, and Nebaj allows you to witness their way of life firsthand and interact with locals who proudly preserve their traditions. By participating in workshops, you can learn traditional arts and crafts, such as weaving and pottery, directly from skilled artisans who pass down these techniques through generations.

Attending festivals and celebrations is another way to immerse yourself in the vibrant Maya culture. One notable example is the "Day of the Dead," known as "Todos Santos" in Guatemala. This annual event, held on November 1st and 2nd, is a deeply significant time when families honor and remember their deceased loved ones. The Maya people believe that during this period, the spirits of the departed return to Earth, and families create intricate altars adorned with flowers, food, and photographs to welcome them. It is a time of both solemn reflection and joyous celebration, as communities come together to honor their ancestors through rituals, music, and traditional foods.

In addition to their spiritual practices and artistic endeavors, Maya communities are renowned for their exceptional craftsmanship. The art of weaving, in particular, holds a special place in Maya culture. Each region boasts its unique weaving style, with distinct patterns and color palettes that reflect the environment and cultural heritage of the community. In the highland town of Chichicastenango, for instance, the women weave vibrant textiles using a backstrap loom, a technique that has been perfected over centuries. These intricately woven fabrics are transformed into clothing, table runners, bags, and other items that are not only beautiful but also carry the stories and traditions of the Maya people.

To fully immerse yourself in the Maya culture, consider participating in homestay programs or community-based tourism initiatives. These experiences allow you to live alongside indigenous families, sharing meals, and engaging in daily activities. By forging personal connections, you gain a deeper appreciation for their way of life, their struggles, and their resilience in preserving their cultural heritage.

Guatemala's vibrant indigenous culture, deeply rooted in the ancient Maya civilization, offers an unparalleled opportunity to witness the living history and traditions of this remarkable civilization. Through their customs, rituals, traditional clothing, and profound connection to nature, the Maya people exemplify the resilience and enduring spirit of Guatemala's indigenous communities. By engaging with and honoring their rich heritage, you not only gain a profound understanding of the Maya culture but also contribute to the preservation and appreciation of Guatemala's diverse indigenous tapestry.

Festivals and Celebrations

Guatemala is renowned for its vibrant festivals and celebrations, which provide a window into the country's cultural heritage and traditions. The calendar of festivities is filled with colorful parades, traditional dances, and lively music, inviting both locals and visitors to immerse themselves in the joyful atmosphere. These events showcase the spirit and passion of the Guatemalan people, offering a unique opportunity to experience the rich tapestry of Guatemala's cultural identity.

One of the most extravagant and widely recognized celebrations in Guatemala is Semana Santa, or Holy Week, which takes place in the colonial city of Antigua. Each year, leading up to Easter, Antigua transforms into a spectacular stage where religious processions, known as "pasos," wind through the cobblestone streets. These pasos feature ornate floats depicting scenes from the Passion of Christ, carried on the shoulders of purple-robed participants. The processions are accompanied by mournful music played by bands called "cucuruchos." This week-long event attracts thousands of visitors who come to witness the solemnity, artistry, and devotion displayed during Semana Santa.

Another mesmerizing festival in Guatemala is the Giant Kite Festival in Sumpango, a small town located in the Sacatepéquez Department. This event, known as "Festival de Barriletes Gigantes," takes place on November 1st, coinciding with the Day of the Dead. The festival pays homage to departed loved ones through the creation and flying of enormous kites. These kites, often measuring up to 20 meters in diameter, are meticulously handcrafted using bamboo frames and colorful tissue paper. Each kite carries intricate designs and messages, reflecting the personal stories and memories associated with those who have passed away. The skies above Sumpango come alive as the kites soar, carrying the hopes and remembrances of the community.

Beyond Semana Santa and the Giant Kite Festival, Guatemala's festive calendar is filled with countless other celebrations that highlight the country's cultural diversity. In Chichicastenango, the town's market square becomes the setting for the Santo Tomás Festival, held in honor of the town's patron saint. Indigenous people from surrounding villages come dressed in their traditional attire to participate in processions, dances, and religious ceremonies. The atmosphere is filled with the sounds of marimba music, the scent of incense, and the vibrant colors of the clothing and decorations.

The Fiesta de la Virgen de Guadalupe, celebrated on December 12th, is another important event in Guatemala. This festival combines Catholic and indigenous beliefs, honoring the Virgin Mary. Processions, fireworks, and cultural performances take place throughout the country, with the main celebration occurring in the Basilica of Esquipulas, a revered pilgrimage site.

In addition to religious festivals, Guatemala also celebrates its indigenous roots through events like the Rabinal Achí Dance Drama. This theatrical performance, recognized as a UNESCO Intangible Cultural Heritage of Humanity, originates from the indigenous community of Rabinal in the Baja Verapaz Department. The dance drama reenacts an ancient Mayan story and combines traditional music, dance, and vibrant costumes. It is a captivating and symbolic representation of Mayan culture and heritage.

One cannot overlook the Festival Folklórico de Cobán, held in the city of Cobán, Alta Verapaz. This festival showcases the cultural diversity of Guatemala, with performances featuring traditional dances, music, and costumes from various regions of the country. It is an opportunity to witness the unique traditions and customs of different indigenous groups, such as the Q'eqchi', Poqomchi', and Achi.

These festivals and celebrations in Guatemala hold deep historical and cultural significance. They serve as a bridge between the past and the present, weaving together indigenous beliefs, Catholic traditions, and the country's complex history. They are not just events for entertainment, but rather an expression of identity, a reflection of cultural resilience, and a means to honor ancestral customs.

Participating in these celebrations offers a firsthand experience of the energy and excitement that permeate the streets during these festive occasions. It allows visitors to connect with the Guatemalan people and gain a deeper understanding of their cultural values, traditions, and way of life. The festivals provide an opportunity to witness the artistry and craftsmanship that goes into creating intricate costumes, giant kites, and religious processions. Moreover, they offer a glimpse into the profound spirituality, resilience, and sense of community that characterizes Guatemala's cultural heritage.

Whether it's the grandeur of Semana Santa, the soaring kites of Sumpango, or the vibrant dances of Cobán, Guatemala's festivals and celebrations offer an immersive and unforgettable experience. They are a testament to the country's rich cultural mosaic, where diverse traditions harmoniously blend and create a vibrant tapestry of Guatemala's identity. By participating in these festivities, visitors can celebrate alongside the Guatemalan people, forging connections and creating lasting memories that embody the true essence of Guatemala's cultural heritage.

Handicrafts and Textiles

Guatemala's handicrafts and textiles hold a special place in the country's cultural landscape, embodying a rich tradition of artistry and heritage. Passed down through generations, these crafts reflect the stories, beliefs, and ancestral wisdom of the indigenous communities that call Guatemala home. In this section, we invite you to explore the fascinating world of traditional crafts and weaving techniques that have been preserved for centuries.

The art of weaving is deeply ingrained in Guatemalan culture, and it serves as a powerful medium of expression for indigenous communities. Each textile is a masterpiece, painstakingly created with intricate designs and symbolism that convey a wealth of meaning. From the vibrant hues to the detailed patterns, every element of Mayan textiles tells a story.

One of the most iconic garments in Guatemalan culture is the huipil, a traditional blouse worn by women. Huipiles are woven with precision and care, often taking months to complete. These beautiful garments showcase the region-specific designs and motifs that distinguish one community from another. For example, the intricate brocade patterns of the K'iche' Maya in the highlands differ from the vibrant geometric designs of the Ixil Maya in the Nebaj region. Each pattern holds significance, representing elements of nature, cosmology, or ancestral lineage.

The weaving process itself is a remarkable feat of craftsmanship. Indigenous women, known as ajk'ijab' (weavers), utilize backstrap looms, a traditional form of loom that has been used for centuries. The backstrap loom is simple in design, consisting of two horizontal bars and a strap that is tied around the weaver's waist. This allows for precise tension control and flexibility, enabling the creation of intricate patterns.

Natural dyes play a vital role in Mayan textile production, further enhancing their cultural significance. Many communities still use traditional methods to extract vibrant colors from natural sources such as plants, insects, and minerals. For instance, the cochineal insect, found on cacti, produces a deep red dye that has been used for centuries. The blue color comes from the añil plant, while shades of yellow are derived from various flowers and roots. These natural dyes not only create a stunning color palette but also reflect a deep connection to the surrounding environment.

Beyond huipiles, Guatemala's handicraft traditions extend to a variety of other textile creations. Intricately woven tapestries, known as cortes, depict stories and historical events. These large-scale textiles often serve as a canvas for communal narratives, portraying the collective memory of a community or conveying the struggles and triumphs of their ancestors.

Artisans also produce an array of accessories, including belts, bags, and hats, adorned with the same meticulous attention to detail. The artistry extends to the use of embroidery, beadwork, and decorative techniques that add depth and texture to these pieces. The skill and creativity of Guatemalan artisans shine through in every stitch, showcasing their ability to transform simple materials into works of art.

To truly appreciate Guatemala's handicrafts and textiles, it is essential to engage with the communities where these traditions are still thriving. Throughout the country, there are numerous cooperatives and workshops that provide opportunities to meet talented artisans and witness their craft firsthand. These encounters offer a glimpse into the lives and stories of the weavers, fostering a deeper appreciation for their work.

In towns like Chichicastenango, Sololá, and Santiago Atitlán, you can visit bustling markets where textiles take center stage. The vibrant colors and intricate patterns of the textiles on display are a visual feast for the senses. Chatting with the artisans, you'll gain insights into their techniques, inspirations, and the cultural significance embedded in their craft. You might even have the chance to witness a demonstration of backstrap weaving, observing the weaver's deft hands as they bring a textile to life.

Beyond the markets, some communities offer immersive experiences where you can learn traditional weaving techniques directly from skilled artisans. Participating in workshops allows you to gain a deeper understanding of the weaving process, from preparing the threads to mastering the intricate patterns. Under the guidance of a patient mentor, you'll gain a newfound appreciation for the precision and skill required to create these magnificent textiles.

By supporting local artisans and cooperatives, you contribute to the preservation of these cultural traditions and help empower indigenous communities. The income generated from the sale of handicrafts provides economic opportunities and helps sustain the weaving traditions for future generations. Every purchase becomes a tangible connection to Guatemala's rich cultural heritage.

Guatemala's handicrafts and textiles are a testament to the skill, creativity, and resilience of its people. They serve as tangible expressions of cultural identity, bridging the past and present, and creating a vibrant tapestry that weaves together the diverse threads of Guatemalan society. As you delve into the world of these extraordinary crafts, may you be inspired by the stories and traditions they encapsulate, and may you cherish the beauty and cultural significance they represent.

Immersion in Local Culture and Traditions

To truly experience Guatemala's cultural heritage, immerse yourself in the local culture and traditions. Engaging in community-based tourism initiatives is an excellent way to have authentic and meaningful interactions with indigenous communities and contribute to their well-being. These initiatives provide opportunities to participate in workshops and demonstrations where you can learn traditional arts, crafts, and culinary practices directly from the skilled artisans.

For example, you can visit the village of San Antonio Aguas Calientes, known for its intricate textile production. Here, you can join a weaving workshop led by local women who have mastered the ancient art of backstrap weaving. They will patiently guide you through the process of preparing the loom, selecting vibrant threads, and weaving intricate patterns. As you sit side by side with these talented weavers, you'll gain a newfound appreciation for the craftsmanship and dedication that goes into creating the traditional garments and accessories.

Additionally, consider participating in traditional cooking classes. In towns like Chichicastenango or Nebaj, you can learn how to prepare authentic Mayan dishes using traditional cooking methods and local ingredients. Under the guidance of experienced cooks, you'll discover the secrets behind the unique flavors and techniques that make Guatemalan cuisine so special. From grinding maize to making tortillas by hand, you'll get a hands-on experience that connects you with the culinary traditions passed down through generations.

To further immerse yourself in the local culture, it's highly recommended to join in ceremonies and rituals that offer a glimpse into the spiritual beliefs and practices of the Maya people. For example, in the village of Santiago Atitlán, you can witness the ancient Mayan ceremony known as the "Maximon" or "Rilaj Mam." Maximon is a spiritual figure representing both good and evil, and the ceremony involves offerings of tobacco, alcohol, and candles, accompanied by prayers and blessings. By observing and respectfully participating in these rituals, you gain a deeper understanding of the spiritual significance and the vital role they play in the community's daily life.

Moreover, engaging in conversations with community leaders and elders is a valuable way to learn about the customs, challenges, and aspirations of the indigenous communities. Take the opportunity to sit down with a Maya elder and listen to their stories and wisdom. They can share anecdotes about their traditions, history, and the changes they have witnessed over the years. Through these interactions, you'll gain insights into the struggles and resilience of these communities, as well as their ongoing efforts to preserve their cultural heritage in the face of modern challenges.

By immersing yourself in the local culture, you forge genuine connections with the people and create lasting memories that will stay with you long after your visit. These experiences also contribute to the preservation of Guatemala's rich heritage. The income generated from community-based tourism initiatives directly supports the indigenous communities, allowing them to maintain their traditional practices and pass them on to future generations. By actively engaging with and supporting these communities, you become a part of their efforts to safeguard their cultural identity and ensure its continuity.

As you explore Guatemala's cultural and indigenous heritage, you'll come to appreciate the immense diversity and depth of the country's traditions. Each community has its own unique customs, languages, and art forms that reflect its distinct history and environment. By immersing yourself in these cultural experiences, you'll gain a profound appreciation for the resilience, creativity, and spiritual richness of the Maya people and other indigenous groups.

Ultimately, your journey through Guatemala's cultural heritage is an opportunity to not only learn and discover but also to contribute positively to the preservation and promotion of these invaluable traditions. It is a chance to form connections, broaden your perspective, and carry with you the profound insights gained from engaging with the vibrant tapestry of Guatemala's cultural legacy.

Through Mayan traditions, festive celebrations, intricate handicrafts, and immersive cultural experiences, Guatemala's Cultural and Indigenous Heritage chapter invites you to appreciate the depth and diversity of the country's cultural tapestry.

Conclusion

In conclusion, exploring Guatemala is a remarkable journey that offers a wealth of unforgettable experiences. From the moment you set foot in this Central American gem, you are greeted by a tapestry of captivating landscapes, each more awe-inspiring than the last. Whether it's the verdant highlands, mist-covered mountains, pristine lakes, or lush rainforests, Guatemala's natural beauty is bound to leave a lasting impression.

Throughout this travel guide, we have embarked on a virtual tour of the diverse regions that make up Guatemala's tapestry. We started in the bustling streets of Guatemala City, where modernity and history converge. Here, the ancient meets the contemporary, with grand colonial architecture coexisting alongside sleek skyscrapers. Exploring the historic Zone 1, with its impressive landmarks and vibrant markets, immerses you in the pulse of urban life in Guatemala.

As we ventured beyond the city, we discovered the timeless charm of Antigua Guatemala. This UNESCO World Heritage Site enchants visitors with its cobblestone streets, colorful facades, and beautifully preserved colonial architecture. Wandering through the city's quaint plazas, you can't help but feel a sense of stepping back in time. The grandeur of the ancient churches, such as the iconic La Merced and San Francisco, tells tales of Antigua's rich religious heritage.

No visit to Guatemala is complete without experiencing the ethereal beauty of Lake Atitlán and its surrounding villages. Nestled among towering volcanoes, this breathtaking lake reflects the vibrant culture of the indigenous communities residing along its shores. Each village boasts its own distinct character and traditions, allowing you to immerse yourself in the daily lives of the Mayan people. From Santiago Atitlán's vibrant textiles to San Marcos La Laguna's spiritual retreats, the villages offer a glimpse into Guatemala's profound indigenous heritage.

Tikal, a crown jewel of Guatemala's ancient Maya civilization, awaits adventurers in the country's northern jungles. Exploring this vast archaeological site is akin to stepping into a lost world. The towering pyramids, intricately carved stelae, and sprawling plazas tell the story of a civilization that thrived centuries ago. As you ascend one of the ancient temples, such as Temple IV, you are rewarded with a breathtaking panoramic view of the surrounding rainforest canopy, a reminder of the symbiotic relationship between the Maya and their natural surroundings.

For those seeking relaxation and beachside bliss, Guatemala's Pacific Coast offers a myriad of options. From the lively beach towns of Monterrico and El Paredón to the secluded paradise of Livingston, the coast entices sun-seekers and surfers alike. Wildlife enthusiasts can explore the protected mangroves of the Pacific Coast, home to an array of bird species, turtles, and even crocodiles. Along the shore, fishermen cast their nets, providing a glimpse into the coastal communities' way of life.

Throughout our journey, we have discovered that Guatemala is not just a destination; it is a symphony of colors, flavors, and traditions. Vibrant festivals such as Semana Santa (Holy Week) and Día de los Muertos (Day of the Dead) showcase Guatemala's fervent devotion and cultural celebrations. The traditional clothing worn by indigenous communities, with its intricate weavings and vibrant hues, tells stories of ancestral customs and identity.

And let's not forget about the mouthwatering cuisine that tantalizes the taste buds. Whether indulging in a hearty plate of pepián, a traditional Mayan stew, or savoring the rich flavors of coffee grown in the Guatemalan highlands, the culinary delights of Guatemala are sure to leave you yearning for more.

By immersing ourselves in the colors, flavors, and wonders of Guatemala, we have gained a deeper understanding and appreciation for this remarkable destination. But perhaps the most treasured aspect of Guatemala is its warm-hearted people. Throughout our journey, we have encountered locals who welcomed us with open arms, sharing their stories, traditions, and laughter. It is their genuine warmth and hospitality that truly make Guatemala a place to remember.

So, whether you seek ancient ruins, breathtaking landscapes, vibrant cultures, or simply a chance to connect with the warmth of humanity, Guatemala promises to be an unforgettable travel experience. As you embark on your own adventure, armed with the knowledge and insights from this travel guide, may you discover the magic that lies within the heart of this captivating country.

Appendix: Useful Phrases and Vocabulary

The appendix section of the Guatemala Travel Guide is designed to provide readers with a comprehensive compilation of useful phrases and vocabulary that can greatly enhance their experience while traveling in Guatemala. From basic greetings to essential words for communication, transportation-related terms, and phrases for navigating various situations, this appendix serves as a valuable reference for meaningful interactions throughout your journey.

Common Greetings:
Mastering basic greetings is a fantastic way to connect with locals and demonstrate respect for the local culture. Here are a few common greetings in Spanish, the official language of Guatemala:

- Hola (Hello)
- Buenos días (Good morning)
- Buenas tardes (Good afternoon)
- Buenas noches (Good evening/night)
- ¿Cómo estás? (How are you?)
- Mucho gusto (Nice to meet you)
- Adiós (Goodbye)
- ¿Qué tal? (How's it going?)
- ¿Cómo te llamas? (What's your name?)
- ¿De dónde eres? (Where are you from?)
- ¿Cómo ha sido tu día? (How has your day been?)
- ¡Bienvenido/a! (Welcome!)
- ¿En qué puedo ayudarte? (How can I help you?)
- Nos vemos luego. (See you later.)

- ¿Cuál es tu comida favorita? (What's your favorite food?)
- ¡Feliz cumpleaños! (Happy birthday!)
- ¿Qué te trae a Guatemala? (What brings you to Guatemala?)
- ¿Dónde puedo encontrar un buen café? (Where can I find a good coffee?)
- ¿Podría recomendar un buen restaurante por aquí? (Could you recommend a good restaurant around here?)
- ¿Cuál es el mejor lugar para ver el atardecer? (What's the best place to watch the sunset?)
- ¡Que tengas un buen día! (Have a nice day!)
- ¿Qué actividades turísticas recomendarías en esta área? (What tourist activities would you recommend in this area?)
- ¿Sabes dónde puedo comprar souvenirs? (Do you know where I can buy souvenirs?)
- ¿Puedes explicarme cómo llegar a la estación de autobuses? (Can you explain to me how to get to the bus station?)
- ¿Cuál es la especialidad culinaria de esta región? (What is the culinary specialty of this region?)
- ¿Sabes de algún lugar interesante para hacer senderismo? (Do you know of any interesting places for hiking?)
- ¿Qué tal es el clima en esta época del año? (What's the weather like this time of year?)

Basic Phrases for Communication:
Having a few key phrases at your disposal can help you navigate daily interactions with ease. Here are some essential phrases for communication:

- Por favor (Please)

- Gracias (Thank you)
- De nada (You're welcome)
- ¿Hablas inglés? (Do you speak English?)
- No entiendo (I don't understand)
- ¿Puede ayudarme? (Can you help me?)
- Disculpe (Excuse me)
- ¿Cuál es tu nombre? (What is your name?)
- ¿Dónde está el baño? (Where is the bathroom?)
- ¿Podría darme indicaciones? (Could you give me directions?)
- ¿Qué recomiendas visitar en esta ciudad? (What do you recommend visiting in this city?)
- ¿Cuánto cuesta esto? (How much does this cost?)
- Me gustaría ordenar... (I would like to order...)
- ¿Aceptan tarjetas de crédito? (Do you accept credit cards?)
- ¿Dónde puedo encontrar un cajero automático? (Where can I find an ATM?)
- ¿Cuándo abre/cierra? (When does it open/close?)
- ¿Hay algún supermercado cerca? (Is there a supermarket nearby?)
- ¿Puedo tomar fotos aquí? (Can I take photos here?)
- ¿Cuál es la especialidad de la casa? (What is the specialty of the house?)
- ¿Dónde puedo comprar recuerdos? (Where can I buy souvenirs?)
- ¿Cuál es el horario de autobuses? (What is the bus schedule?)
- ¿Qué actividades hay para hacer en esta zona? (What activities are there to do in this area?)
- ¿Puedo obtener un mapa de la ciudad? (Can I get a map of the city?)
- ¿Qué hora es? (What time is it?)
- ¿Cuánto tiempo se tarda en llegar a...? (How long does it take to get to...?)

- ¿Dónde puedo encontrar información turística? (Where can I find tourist information?)
- ¿Qué tipo de clima hace aquí en esta época del año? (What kind of weather is it here at this time of year?)

Transportation-Related Vocabulary:
Getting around Guatemala efficiently requires familiarity with transportation-related vocabulary. Here are some useful terms to know:

- Autobús (Bus)
- Taxi (Taxi)
- Estación de autobuses (Bus station)
- Aeropuerto (Airport)
- Tren (Train)
- Parada (Stop)
- Billete/boleto (Ticket)
- Colectivo (Shared minibus)
- Vehículo (Vehicle)
- Terminal de autobuses (Bus terminal)
- Vuelo (Flight)
- Equipaje (Luggage)
- Andén (Platform)
- Hora de salida (Departure time)
- Hora de llegada (Arrival time)
- Pasaporte (Passport)
- Migración (Immigration)
- Control de seguridad (Security check)
- Embarque (Boarding)
- Asiento (Seat)
- Descuento (Discount)
- Parqueo (Parking)
- Estación de tren (Train station)
- Horario (Schedule)

- Servicio de transporte (Transportation service)
- Pregunta al conductor (Ask the driver)
- ¿Dónde está la parada más cercana? (Where is the nearest stop?)
- ¿Cuánto cuesta? (How much does it cost?)
- ¿A dónde va este autobús? (Where does this bus go?)

Essential Words for Navigating Situations:
Being able to navigate various situations confidently is key to a smooth travel experience. Here are some essential words to help you in different scenarios:

- Restaurante (Restaurant)
- Menú (Menu)
- Comida (Food)
- Bebida (Drink)
- Baño (Bathroom)
- Farmacia (Pharmacy)
- Emergencia (Emergency)
- Ayuda (Help)
- Mapa (Map)
- Hotel (Hotel)
- Habitación (Room)
- Reservación (Reservation)
- Recepción (Reception)
- Check-in/Check-out
- Transporte (Transportation)
- Aerolínea (Airline)
- Estación de tren (Train station)
- Puerto (Port)
- Excursión (Excursion)
- Guía turístico (Tour guide)
- Tarjeta de crédito (Credit card)
- Dinero en efectivo (Cash)

- Mercado (Market)
- Artesanía (Handicraft)
- Souvenir (Souvenir)
- Parque Nacional (National Park)
- Aventura (Adventure)
- Playa (Beach)
- Fotografía (Photography)
- Internet/Wi-Fi (Internet/Wi-Fi)

In addition to these practical phrases and vocabulary, let's dive deeper into a few cultural nuances and anecdotes that can further enrich your interactions while traveling in Guatemala:

Politeness and Respect:
Guatemalan culture places a strong emphasis on politeness and respect, and incorporating these values into your interactions will be greatly appreciated. When engaging with locals, using phrases like "por favor" (please) and "gracias" (thank you) can go a long way in creating a positive impression. These simple words convey appreciation and gratitude, fostering a friendly atmosphere. Additionally, addressing people with their appropriate titles, such as "señor" (sir) or "señora" (madam), demonstrates respect and acknowledgment of their age or position. This cultural sensitivity helps to establish a harmonious connection with the locals and showcases your understanding of their customs.

Local Cuisine Adventures:
Guatemala boasts a diverse and flavorful culinary scene, and exploring local cuisine is an adventure in itself. When dining at local restaurants, a few well-chosen phrases can enhance your culinary experience. For instance, when ordering food, you can say, "Me gustaría probar un plato típico de Guatemala" (I would like to try a typical Guatemalan dish).

This shows your genuine interest in the local gastronomy and may prompt the server to recommend their specialty or provide insights into regional favorites. Don't hesitate to inquire about the ingredients or flavors of a particular dish. Guatemalans take pride in their culinary heritage and are often delighted to share information and stories behind their traditional recipes.

Seeking Directions and Exploring:
As you navigate the streets and landmarks of Guatemala, there may be instances when you need to ask for directions. When approaching locals for help, it's important to maintain a polite and respectful attitude. Begin by saying, "Disculpe, ¿podría indicarme cómo llegar a..." (Excuse me, could you tell me how to get to...), followed by the name of your destination or landmark. This polite inquiry is likely to elicit a helpful response, as Guatemalans are known for their friendliness and willingness to assist travelers. Whether it's finding your way to a historical site or locating a local market, locals are often happy to guide you with a smile and may even offer additional tips or recommendations to enhance your journey.

Engaging in Conversations:
One of the most rewarding aspects of traveling in Guatemala is the opportunity to engage in conversations with locals. This opens doors to unique insights into Guatemalan culture, traditions, and daily life. To initiate meaningful conversations, consider asking open-ended questions that invite locals to share their experiences and stories. For example, you could inquire about the significance of a traditional festival by asking, "¿Cómo se celebra la fiesta tradicional en esta región?" (How is the traditional festival celebrated in this region?). This shows genuine interest in their customs and allows locals to share their knowledge, anecdotes, and personal connections to these cultural

celebrations. As you engage in these conversations, you may find yourself invited to participate in festivities or discover hidden gems that may not be found in guidebooks, providing you with a truly immersive and authentic experience of Guatemala.

Remember, while the appendix serves as a valuable reference, it's essential to approach interactions with an open mind, curiosity, and a willingness to learn. Guatemalans are known for their warmth and hospitality, and by making an effort to communicate in their language and show respect for their culture, you'll forge deeper connections and create lasting memories during your travels in this beautiful country.

Printed in Great Britain
by Amazon